Prosperity Principles

52 Keys to Personal and Practice Success for Chiropractors

Jeri Anderson, DC

Darci Stotts, DC

Patty Dominguez

The Indie Doctors Media

Copyright © 2019 The Indie Doctors Media

All rights reserved.

ISBN-13: 9781796852295

PRAISE FOR PROSPERITY PRINCIPLES

"Whether you are a student, new in practice or a seasoned veteran, you will want "Prosperity Principles" in your library. Dr. Anderson and Dr. Stotts have created a pool of wisdom for you to draw from."

-Dr. George B. Curry
Windsor, CT
Past President, International Chiropractors Association

* * * *

"Darci and Jeri have put together an excellent collection of valuable insights not only into the creation of a successful chiropractic healing practice, but also into living a happy and successful life. This book will bring useful tools to help both doctors at the beginnings of their career but also to well-established practitioners who may be plateauing. I think this is a gathering of wisdom rarely found within the covers of one book and which will reward rereading often."

- Kevin Proudman, DC
Derry, Northern Ireland
Past President of the United Chiropractic Association

* * * *

"Prosperity Principles is a great guide not only to start you off in practice but also to get you back on track with your practice and life. Simple, easy to follow, practical steps that can be repeated year after year."

-Melissa Sanford
Brighton, UK
CEO, United Chiropractic Association, United Kingdom

"Prosperity Principles is a modern approach to the daily challenges of practice. I appreciate that each chapter is written on different subjects, and all build on each other. This will be the 'go-to' book for fresh knowledge and advice on everyday practice challenges and will keep you on track to a successful practice. Thank you, Dr. Darci, Dr. Jeri, and Patty for collaborating and creating this powerful tool for chiropractors to take their practice to the next level!"

-Lavonne Pineda, DC
San Jose, CA
#1 Amazon International bestselling author of Decoding Pelvic Pain

* * * *

"Wow! If only this had been written 15 years ago. So many golden nuggets. Whether you are a newly qualified DC or an experienced DC this book has something for all of us. So much information collated in one place by reputable practitioners who work in the field. Ready to be imbibed. They have combined with their own take for us to reap the rewards. Whether you digest one chapter a day, or binge all at once, the return on value for the time spent reading will exceed your expectations. Invest your time and money. The Prosperity Principles won't disappoint."

-Mary Phillips, DC
Douglas, Isle of Man

"Prosperity principles provides those who want to succeed in the chiropractic BUSINESS a step by step guide of details the struggling chiropractor takes for granted. While reading this book I thought it was written specifically for me! Obviously written by someone who is thoughtful enough to want others to succeed. The chapters are easy to follow but jammed with information. This book is the "Think and Grow Rich" for chiropractors on the up and down rollercoaster. Should be mandatory reading for students or battle scared doctors, because it will change your headspace."

- Brian Norce, DC
Coeur D'Alene, ID

* * * *

"Prosperity Principles is an excellent step- by- step guide to making things happen. Dr. Jeri's and Dr. Darci's words are uplifting, smart, witty, and full of knowledge and inspiration. Whether you are a student, new grad, seasoned doc, or somewhere in between, Prosperity Principles is a must read for all; full of priceless information that is guaranteed to lift you up and get you moving. It will give you the guidance and motivation needed to reach your goals and attain the success you deserve. If you're looking for positive vibes and a wealth of knowledge, this is the book for you."

- Britni Everett, DC
Bellevue, WA

DEDICATIONS

To my three greatest mentors, who are now my angels, I am so grateful and will love you forever. To my friends and advisors who have supported me in this project, thank you! And to my critics, I love you and thank you as well. To every chiropractor that is seeking success, this book is for you!

- Jeri

To my prosperity teacher, Dr. Rolla J. Pennell, DC.

Love, Darci

Thank you first and foremost to my esteemed docs and dear friends, Drs. Anderson & Stotts. When I met them, while they have a calm demeanor, make no mistake, they have zero tolerance for any bullsh*t. I respect that tremendously. When I heard about their big vision of elevating the chiropractic space, I knew it was something that I could get behind. They are truly a force individually and together, well you can 10x that into the stratosphere of awesome. It is truly my pleasure to have been asked to include some marketing nuggets here within these pages. I hope you take action on what you read here because these concepts work! Lastly, and as always, thank you to my family for always being so supportive of me. I get to live my dharma and passion everyday which is to help others create greater impact for their legacy, which is my legacy.

-Patty

Table of Contents

PRAISE FOR PROSPERITY PRINCIPLES

DEDICATIONS

Introduction

Chapter 1
32,000 FEET OF EXPANSION _____ 4

Chapter 2
TREASURED _____ 8

Chapter 3
THROW THIS NEW PATIENT OUT OR KEEP THEM? _____ 12

Chapter 4
TWO SETS OF FACTS _____ 16

Chapter 5
MARKETING TRUTH #1: IF YOU THINK YOUR MARKETING SUCKS, HERE'S WHAT TO DO ABOUT IT... _____ 20

Chapter 6
CHANGE SOMETHING ...ANYTHING! _____ 26

Chapter 7
WHY DON'T ALL NEW PATIENTS CONVERT TO CARE? _____ 30

Chapter 8
ARE YOU LISTENING? _____ 36

Chapter 9
MARKETING TRUTH #2: SCARCITY... IS A GOOD THING _____ 40

Chapter 10
BRING BACK THE WONDER _____ 44

Chapter 11
CHIROPRACTIC P R O S P E R I T Y _____ 48

Chapter 12
THE PERFECT PRACTICE _____ 52

Chapter 13
MARKETING TRUTH #3: PRICING LIKE A PRO _____ 56

Chapter 14
DO YOU TESLA? _____ 60

Chapter 15
DON'T BE AN ISLAND _____ 64

Chapter 16
BEING CERTAIN _____ 68

Chapter 17
CATCH SUCCESS _____ 72

Chapter 18
MARKETING TRUTH #4: MESSAGING MATTERS _____ 76

Chapter 19
BUST A RUT _____ 80

Chapter 20
THE ADJUSTMENT IS #1!! _____ 84

Chapter 21
LOOKING FOR THE NEXT SHINEY OBJECT _____ 88

Chapter 22
SUPERLATIVE CERTIFIED _____ 92

Chapter 23
MARKETING TRUTH #5: MARKETING THAT WENT OUT
WITH THE MULLET _____ 96

Chapter 24
WHY? NO REALLY...WHY? _____ 100

Chapter 25
FAILURE TO PLAN, PLANNING TO FAIL _____ 104

Chapter 26
LEVERAGING DISAPPOINTMENTS _____ 106

Chapter 27
COVET YOUR LICENSE AND STAY OUT OF JAIL_____110

Chapter 28
TECHNIQUE _____114

Chapter 29
MARKETING TRUTH #6: THE THREE WAYS TO GROW YOUR BUSINESS _____118

Chapter 30
INITIATE INTENTION _____ 122

Chapter 31
IF YOU WEAR OUT YOUR BODY, WHERE ARE YOU GOING TO LIVE?_____ 126

Chapter 32
OWN IT! _____ 130

Chapter 33
MOOD RING MANAGEMENT _____ 134

Chapter 34
MARKETING TRUTH #7: BE REMARKABLE _____ 138

Chapter 35
CREATING A TEAM SWEET SPOT _____ 142

Chapter 36
LIKE STEVE MCQUEEN… _____ 146

Chapter 37
PULL THAT RIPCORD! _____ 150

Chapter 38
MARKETING TRUTH #8: HOW TO CREATE AN OFFER, THE RIGHT WAY! _____ 154

Chapter 39
CREATING F R E E D O M _____ 158

Chapter 40
IF ALL YOU HAVE IS A HAMMER, THEN EVERYTHING IS A NAIL _____ 162

Chapter 41
HEADSPACE 101 _____ 164

Chapter 42
MARKETING TRUTH #9: JUST ASK. _____ 168

Chapter 43
BE AFRAID, VERY AFRAID OF THE SCARCITY MINDSET _____ 172

Chapter 44
DO YOU HAVE A STAFF INFECTION? _____ 176

Chapter 45
THE LONG VIEW _____ 180

Chapter 46
DON'T HIRE CHELSEA _____ 184

Chapter 47
THE WORD "CLOSE" IN CHIROPRACTIC _____ 188

Chapter 48
AWAKEN THE SLEEPING GIANT _____ 194

Chapter 49
RELENTLESS _____ 198

Chapter 50
GOIN' NOWHERE? _____ 202

Chapter 51
NUTS AND BOLTS CHECK LIST_____ 206

Chapter 52
WHERE DO YOU GO FROM HERE? _____ 214

ABOUT THE AUTHORS

Introduction

First of all, THANK YOU for joining us in Prosperity Principles!

So, why are you reading this book? And what do you wish to gain from it? If you hadn't already guessed, we're going to ask you lots of questions along our journey together in the pages that follow.

You see, we wrote this book to open your perspective, sharpen your vision and to begin a path to Health, Peace and Freedom for you and yours.

Why did we write this? Simple, because we are tired of watching good doctors struggle and not realize their dreams.

If you wish to complain about chiropractic, argue, criticize, or create more division, this book is not for you.

Together, the authors have over 80 years of combined experience. We wish you could know how many great doctors that we have seen leave the profession and go on to other careers because they got tired of the struggle.

We've witnessed countless doctors that are disillusioned or frustrated and are plugging away in practice with broken spirits. If this is you, read on, you have hope!

If you are a young doctor reading this, great! Let's get you started on the right path to realize your success!

If you've been out of school for a bit and are just not where you'd like to be in practice, read on! Let's open your mind and vision to your prosperity!

If you're re-entering our great profession, then let's join hands and get you back on track to your dreams.

And if you're already highly successful, then read on friend because eagles like to hang out with eagles!

Prosperity Principles started out as a series of blog posts over a year ago. We thought that it would be fun to create one success tip per week for a year, thus 52 tips.

After reading the responses to our posts and being contacted by countless doctors that were resonating with our message and needed help and hope, we began to realize that we should take this seriously and put our thoughts together into one place…namely a book.

Since so many doctors are struggling with getting new patients, we asked our dear friend Patty Dominguez to join us in this endeavor. You may not be familiar with Patty yet, read on please. Patty is a marketing strategist that is genius in her work. In her corporate days, she oversaw a billion-dollar marketing portfolio. Yes, you read that correctly…a billion dollars.

Together, we have laid out the thought process to chiropractic prosperity. We have shed light on the planning process, and we have set out the questions to ask yourself along the way. While we cannot give you every answer in the space of a book; we can help open the door to your success.

If perhaps we are sometimes redundant in our message, it's by design as we all need consistent reminders to keep us on our success path.

The core values that we would like to share with you are Health, Peace and Freedom. We believe all chiropractors should have all three:

You have nothing without your Health, and we see countless doctors that sacrifice their Health to try to keep their numbers up at their offices. Please docs, no more. We will show you how to put your Health first.

There is no Peace when you are caught up in the day to day struggles. There is no Peace when you are not realizing your dreams. Let's all have Peace. Follow the Prosperity Principles and you'll gain Peace. You must first do the work.

Success done correctly, allows you Freedom, true Freedom. Mentally, from letting go of the struggles, physically from no longer being chained to the office, and financially from having a bank account that allows you to sleep well at night.

So, let's begin our journey together...here's to your success!

Blessings upon blessings,

Dr. Jeri Anderson, DC and Dr. Darci Stotts, DC

Chapter 1
32,000 FEET OF EXPANSION

"My legacy is that I stayed the course…from the beginning to the end, because I believed in something inside of me."
– Tina Turner

As I write this, I'm sitting in first class at 32,000 feet. I often think of a quote that Darci Stotts once shared with me from a mentor of hers. It goes something like this: any luxury experienced three times becomes a necessity. Guilty. I rarely fly in coach.

You see, I believe in expansion versus contraction.

John Lennon sat down to work and said "let's write a swimming pool" when he was doing renovation on his home. Three hours later he and Paul McCartney wrote their mega-hit HELP!, demonstrating that the constructive work that we do turns our dreams and goals into reality.

The truth is that we all need to work. Even if you're independently wealthy, you need to work. We have a duty to contribute to humanity. The question is are you working from an expansive space or a contractive place?

Some of my greatest ideas and work pieces happen in first class. I'm comfortable and my mind is uninterrupted. That's expansion and creativity flows. Work is easy.

Many docs operate out of a place of lack and contraction. Nothing good happens there. For example, I can save some bucks and fly in coach. No problem. And in my discomfort, I don't get crap done. Savings comes at a heavy cost. Contraction. And I work harder when I land.

I have met so many docs that take less than a week's vacation each year. Why? Because they can't afford to leave the office. Perfect contraction mindset. Here's a reality check: you can't afford to stay.

Taking no breaks does not make you more money, it makes you less. You burn out and you get stale. Your patients notice it. Your referrals drop. Your creativity and sense of possibility tanks. You are simply hammering away at NOTHING. Growth doesn't happen in a contractive state.

Have you worked with any Olympic class athletes? Any elite athlete knows that they cannot stay at peak performance year-round. They follow periodized training wherein they plan for performance peaks and corresponding unloading cycles. You are just like an elite athlete in your office: plan for peaks and then get out of the office to unload and expand. Make your work constructive versus destructive.

Our most precious commodity is TIME. I find that few docs truly value time.

Most docs waste time. The best way to leverage your earning capacity is to leverage your time. And the more time you allow yourself to operate your life from an expansive space, the greater your earnings will be and your bank account.

Looking into the year ahead, where can you maximize your expansive space?

Boom, there's a key to your success! You're welcome!

To receive complementary resources to this book including videos, downloads, audios that will support your practice, we invite you to visit:

www.prosperityprinciplesbook.com/resources

This dynamic page will continue to provide updates that are relevant and actionable for you.

Chapter 2
TREASURED

"Love is never wasted..."
- C.S. Lewis

The New Year is out of the gate and you're off and running now. Hopefully you've written down your goals for the year ahead. Now let's get down to business. How are you going to make it happen?

Let's start with what is most treasured in your life and soul. What and/or who would you lay down your life for and cherish until your last breath? Who is let down when you give up too easily? Who or what suffers when you fail to perform?

Every single person treasures SOMETHING: spouse, child, family, partner, faith, health, possessions...

These treasures are your ANCHORS. This is your why. This is why you get up every day and perform to the greatest extent of your abilities. This is why you go the distance and don't give up. This is why you get uncomfortable at times to attain your goals.

We all need ANCHORS. However very few docs actually honor them. It's time for you to acknowledge and honor your treasured anchors.

I bet you're asking how?

You honor what's treasured in your life by keeping those anchors in your vision every single day. Let's say your family is a treasured anchor, then you display their picture in each of your adjusting rooms/areas. My favorite spot is at a location that I can see from the head of the adjusting table so that I'm looking straight at it as I'm adjusting or interacting with a patient. Mine are up on the wall near the ceiling. It's not for decoration. It's not for the patients to see. Frankly, I don't think they ever notice. It's for me.

Placing your ANCHORS at pivotal inconspicuous locations in your office holds you accountable. It reminds you consciously and subconsciously why you do what you do. Placing those reminders allows you to stay focused and to quit farting around wasting precious time. It reminds you to connect with each patient and to make each interaction matter. Because when you fail to deliver you let down not only yourself and your patient, but also what's treasured in your life.

If your desire is to attain your goals this year and beyond, then put what's treasured in your life behind it. Lay it on the line for what matters most. Display your anchors and honor them daily.

Chapter 3

THROW THIS NEW PATIENT OUT OR KEEP THEM?

"Be kind to unkind people. They need it the most."
– Ashleigh Brilliant

Have you ever lived this scenario in your office:

This patient was a total AHole from the beginning. Why did they even show up if they didn't want to be here, fill out the forms and be halfway cordial? They are in tons of pain and act like they can't be put out to sign a few forms! They have been rude, short, cussed, ignored each staff member and made plenty of sarcastic comments.

Why am I wasting my time with this jerk?

How many times has that happened at your office?

Chiropractic tends to attract patients in pain by the droves and often they are seeking some immediate help and relief. I can't blame them. If you think about it and put yourself in that spot, you really would want something similar, right?

The question is are they really a fit for you and your office or are they a better fit somewhere else?

Here's a way to look at it without throwing out the baby with the bath water:

What often happens is that these folks are genuinely sweet, kind people but they have a "thorn in their paw" so to speak.

Remember the story about the lion with a thorn in his paw. Everyone thought he was vicious, and someone took the time to see what was wrong with him and removed the thorn and he was a total sweetheart.

This is often the case and will show up in a visit or two past the first adjustment. It will be very obvious, and you'll be glad you hung in there to pull out the "thorn". The sweetness in a person is sometimes hard to see when pain is covering up their true personality.

I have heard many doctors say that "they are to behave and be nice from the start or that patient is outta here!" The truth is that we are never really ourselves the first time we meet someone and add some moderate pain in there and we definitely aren't ourselves.

We all have had these patients and hung in there and they've become referring machines!

The opposite is true as well. If by the 4 or 5th visit they aren't happy campers, you and your office may not be a fit for them. Time always tells the true story.

Our commitment to care is that we don't judge a patient right off the bat and we give them a chance to show us who they are without the shroud of pain covering their true personalities.

Chapter 4
TWO SETS OF FACTS

"Think like a proton, always positive."
– *Unknown*

In every scenario there are two sets of facts. PI cases are a great example: the patient believes they are hurt and the defense argues that the patient is a liar, a cheat, and a fraud. The jury is left to decide between the two sets of facts.

The funny thing is, your brain works the same way. The only difference is that you often give your brain only one set of facts. Please allow me to explain...

Chiropractors are exposed to many great ideas, coaches, mentors, and web content to help them be successful in practice. There are approximately 60k chiropractors in the United States, do you really think they are all killing it in practice? More than likely not.

Here's why: it is easy to tell your brain that it's too complicated, that you aren't capable, that you're too busy, etc, etc, etc. But that's just one set of facts.

The other set of facts is that you're completely capable and even gifted. (By the way, we are all gifted.) And you can rock your practice, be successful and live the life of your dreams!

The real question is, which set of facts do you give your brain to work on? When we allow ourselves to be successful, we seamlessly move towards success. Now that doesn't mean that we don't have to work...we do have to put in the effort. However, positive effort is perceived differently by the brain than negative effort. One feels empowering and the other feels like dragging a ball and chain.

How do you change? Listen to the thoughts that you tell yourself. Are you a liar, a cheat and a fraud to yourself? Or are you success in progress? When you hear thoughts that are not productive, write them down. Ask yourself: am I 100% completely certain that this is true? Then write down the opposite truth and act on it immediately.

For example: "This is too complicated." Reverse it: "This is easy and I can break it down into simple steps." Next, do step 1 in your project. Give your brain a different set of facts to work with and reinforce it by doing something towards your end goal.

Sometimes success means managing aspects of a project, rather than doing every part. For example: maybe writing sales copy is not your gift. No problem, hire someone to write copy for that part of the project. You manage the project and its outcome. Play to your strengths. The outcome is success. Doing nothing gets you nothing and reinforces your negative thoughts.

Give yourself permission to succeed and give your brain a great set of facts that it can work with! Just like a jury trial, truth is the perception that you assign to it. Once you allow yourself permission to succeed and the perception that it is inevitable, you own success.

Chapter 5

MARKETING TRUTH #1:

IF YOU THINK YOUR MARKETING SUCKS, HERE'S WHAT TO DO ABOUT IT...

*"If you don't know where you are going,
any road will get you there..."*
- Cheshire Cat, Alice in Wonderland

The formula for business success is simple but not easy. At the core, once you have your service/product figured out, your marketing plan should be a natural progression.

In fact, we would challenge the thinking that your business plan and marketing plan are one in the same to a certain extent.

Some small businesses may say, "I don't really need any marketing right now, we are doing alright."

While, you can't argue with a business that has a stable customer base, you have to consider the philosophy that extending the opportunity beyond the first transaction is where the lifetime value of your customer is increased. More sales equals more profits.

After all, marketing is what you do to create awareness for your product or service, and that awareness should be continuous. The beautiful thing about technology and the internet is that it has created a level playing field where small business can act fast, be nimble and gain a respectable position in their niche. Even if you think that your business doesn't qualify to be online... well, you are missing out.

Successful business owners who understand that technology is the great equalizer where any business regardless of size can show up in a way that sets themselves apart. So why is it that some businesses fail with their marketing efforts and would rather remain status quo vs. putting themselves out there with marketing?

Here's the truth: There are no shortcuts to good marketing. In order to win at marketing, you have to have a strategy, a roadmap that provides clarity of the outcome you are seeking.

Imagine throwing puzzle pieces on the table, but having no point of reference of what picture you are creating. No visibility is dangerous and risky. It's no different with marketing that lacks a strategic approach.

Reactive marketing where you "try" something new or listen to a fellow business owner who has had success with a specific tactic is likely to net you mixed results and ultimately can be costly.

When you look at tactical solutions with no correlation back to an overarching strategy, you are setting yourself up for a higher probability of lackluster results — this is where you want to heed caution of marketing service providers who promise the magic bullet of a specific marketing tactic.

Tactics should be considered only one part of the overall marketing outreach puzzle.

Want to create greater connections and build customer loyalty for greater sales and sustainable business growth?

Of course you do, otherwise why would you be in business?

We encourage you to consider the following high-level areas that all marketing strategies should include: Congruency, Relevancy and Nurturing.

Congruency

Congruence is when who you are as a brand, and who you represent yourself to be, is one in the same. Customer loyalty is further strengthened because of congruency. Take a look at your entire business process, from start to finish and ask yourself,

What are my customers experiencing?

Am I showing up as a brand consistently?

Is my brand promise clear?

Do I understand my customer intimately?

Do I know who my perfect customer is?

The point here is that you want to show up congruently. The way to win at congruency is to have a deep understanding of your customer and that your customer is at the center of your business ecosystem. Businesses who understand this, win.

Not sure who your perfect customer is? This is an essential exercise to conduct if you haven't already done so. In about one hour of time, you can put a profile together that puts specificity to your ideal customers demographic, psychographic and behavioral attributes.

Once you have a deep understanding of this profile, then you understand what messaging resonates with them best. Congruency is at the center of this process, because your perfect customer must have a clear understanding of what value you bring. If there are mixed messages, then trust cannot be built.

Relevancy

So now that your perfect customer is clear, what are you going to say to them that make them want to remember? Here is where your marketing relevancy is essential to position yourself as the go-to resource in your market.

We often hear, "but my market is so unique," or, "my market is saturated, there's heavy competition."

Truth is, that may be the case, but that's even more of a reason to understand how to find your uniqueness and then make it relevant to your customer long term. This may come at the risk of you assessing that your business model may have to be tweaked along the way.

Perhaps even a reinvention is in order, whether it's a rebranding or taking a look at your product offering mix. The point here is that staying the same is not an option; business models are in continuous shift, however so subtle.

The option to remain status quo commoditizes your business, so this is a call to action to evolve, to be relevant for the long term.

Nurturing

Lastly, the nurturing process is primarily intended to build deep trust with your customers. This is a long-term play as well in which consistency plays a huge part in finding success with this approach.

Those businesses that try and shortcut this nurturing process ultimately fail and will become the flash in the pan that very few ever remember. Instead, recognize that nurturing means educating your customers to want your business product or service as the solution to their problem.

Thing is, every customer is in a different stage within the buying decision process, and because of that your outreach should be predictably consistent.

Is this sexy? No! It's work, sometimes a lot of work, but the upside is that you are planting digital seeds of knowledge and value.

Your "point of view" marketing should provide answers to common questions in which you can position yourself as the expert.

Will you convert every prospect into a customer? Maybe not, but you will increase the probability of establishing yourself as an authority.

Understanding the power of congruency, relevancy and nurturing is a strategic approach that will provide your customers a solid foundation to build trust, buy from you and tell others.

In the process, you will position yourself for critical mindshare in your perfect customer's mind. Position yourself to win with these foundational principles for business success.

Chapter 6

CHANGE SOMETHING ...ANYTHING!

"I always wondered why somebody doesn't do something about that. Then I realized I was somebody."
– Lily Tomlin

When what you do doesn't seem to be getting the patient better in the appropriate amount of time, you **must** do something different. You will effectively lose that patient forever if you don't and you will shortchange chiropractic. Chiropractic is awesome.... there is a path for most patients to get better. You must be the leader and director to find that path for them. It may not be what you dreamed of doing for them initially, but let the ego go and do what is absolutely best for the patient.

I have seen lazy doctors allow this to happen as well: their patient continues on the same care plan without results. It happens all too often, the same ineffective care going on and on and on. STOP and do re-checks, exams, whatever necessary to unlock their lock. You can't allow the pattern of non-responsiveness to continue. The patient loses confidence in you and then you are off their list as their doctor. You can't go backwards from that spot either. You can't repair that very kind of mis-management easily. The patient walks. We all have had patients from other chiropractic offices come in and the patient just needed a tad different approach, but the other doctor just didn't go that extra step. They instead allowed the patient to leave! That makes NO sense at all! Get in there and do your job and let go of ego and stop being lazy!

When you think about the consequences of not doing all you can to help the patient, it is startling. They will only have a few options if you think about it. Their perception is that chiropractic doesn't work. They may go home and see if it gets better on its own; this is the least likely circumstance. They were motivated to see someone, so they probably won't just go on home and see how things go. They may go to a physiotherapist. They may go the medical route. If they go the medical route the odds of them ever seeing a chiropractor again is over. More than likely this is the route that they will go because all other options have failed in their minds. That idea should make you **livid**. You have opened the door to medicine that more than likely can't help them, and you've also opened the door to opioids. Don't get me wrong; I am not talking about the patient that needs to be co-managed with a medical doctor. We occasionally have to share a patient with an MD, but it is usually for only a short period of time and then they are back in our office full time.

Let's say you can't figure out what to do next? What about a second opinion? Medical doctors do second opinions all the time. Chiropractors almost never do. How sad. You probably have a colleague down the road that would love to help. Chiropractic will move forward when we learn how to better work together and leverage our differences rather than fight over them. Collaboration is a 10x win for our patients and our chiropractic family.

Ultimately, we can deliver the best care possible when we are always looking for the best answers for our patients and producing the best clinical responses for them.

Chapter 7

WHY DON'T ALL NEW PATIENTS CONVERT TO CARE?

"Believe in yourself! Have faith in your abilities! Without a humble but reasonable confidence in your own powers you cannot be successful or happy."
– *Norman Vincent Peale*

Over and over we see new patients at our office and they totally get the concept of chiropractic and commit to care and even refer new patients to our offices. Then we have the certain percentage of patients that do not convert to care.

Why does this happen when we say the same things, we show them x-rays with similar explanations, we show them the same fee schedule and then they walk out?

For some doctors this isn't just a sometime event; sadly, it's a very common, day to day occurrence.

Those common experiences are the ones I am referring to today.

We can say that the new patient didn't have money, or they just didn't have the time. Those are both reasons why someone doesn't buy chiropractic. It happens to us all in small percentages and, ultimately, they may end up coming back and starting care later.

The times when the new patient has money and no time or schedule objections, they should commit to care without a hitch, but they don't. Why don't they then? What is the answer to this question?

We must look at the common denominator in these situations and that would be the doctor. The doctor has several common qualities that make a patient want to get care, and several commonalities that makes a patient run for the hills.

It's really common for us to judge a patient's ability to commit to care. We decide whether they can pay or whether they have time, almost instantly for some random reason.

We all try not to, but it still happens.

That alone will change what our demeanor is like and even how we present the information to the patient. There is no doubt that an astute patient will pick up on this and they will sit back and not get the value of chiropractic. Sadly, they walk out and another patient is lost for our team and the medical team is warming up for the home run.

In my mind, the number one reason patients don't convert to chiropractic care still has to do with the doctor. The answer is the doctor's confidence.

We can posture, we can beat our chests after an easy win, but do we really analyze why we struck out on a seemingly simple new patient conversion? When we are honest with ourselves, we can see clearly it has to do with our confidence.

The good news is that the three things that hold doctors back in the confidence area are fixable.

First, we lose focus on what we are aiming for with the report. Second, we then fall down the hill and lose momentum with the patient. You'll hear the mini agreements stop, you'll hear the questions in their voice. Their voice changes and it's a subtle inflection change but it happens all the time. You'll see the patient sit back with their arms crossed.

The patient is now disconnected, and they need a reason to reconnect and often they really are looking for a reason to reconnect. The third and fatal mistake: We typically offer them clinical information instead of re-connecting, this is cold and sterile to a new patient.

Losing focus, getting disconnected and not reconnecting with rapport are the reasons the lack of confidence in the doctor appears. We innately know when it's happening, and we go to the logical route to fix it, and then we for sure swing at a ball instead of a strike.

We can't reconnect with our new patient with clinical information. The patient is human, and they want a human on the other end to tell them what is in it for them. How is this care going to make "life changing things happen?", is really what they want to know.

They don't need to hear how much the atlas is subluxated and how the instrument is going to correct it and zero is the greatest place to be ever!! NO. They will not be able to relate to that explanation at all, and truly that conversation is all about the doctor anyway.

Do I look at measurements and angles and vectors for patients? Absolutely. That is all clinical and it is not for the lay person and totally confuses the patient. I am not saying that the patient isn't smart. They are incredibly bright, that is why they are at your office! They do not need the clinical explanation of your technique though.

Does your mechanic explain how your carburetor works and then tell you how they repaired it so that you'll have confidence in their work? Of course NOT! Why do we do that same thing though expecting a different result? Lack of confidence is my answer.

Boosting up your confidence is not a matter of flexing and standing in front of the mirror giving yourself a pep talk. The way you change it is to change the way you think. You can keep your focus on the patient and your confidence will change naturally. It is all about them and we will improve our confidence instantly when we do put them first.

The third factor that holds doctors back is that you can't have a "lack of" mentality when you go into the report. "I really need this money/patient", or "I really would have more confidence if I converted this patient". This will perpetuate the problem and give you more of the same.

Before you go into the report, think of all the reasons why this patient needs care so desperately?

Most patients don't even know these reasons half of the time. We can see the future much clearer than they can regarding the consequences of not getting care. We have to go into the report focusing on these reasons. We know that their life depends on it.

Our job is to educate our patients along the way of their healing journey with us, but not on report day. So, if we keep focusing on them the answers will come. For example, if they are very focused on pain and their goal is to remove pain when they arrived, meet them there and they will see what you are offering as a solution.

Our solution for our patient must be a match to what their goals are when they walk into our office. Of course, we know there's more to chiropractic than just getting rid of pain, but we can't bring them up to our speed on their first experience. It is totally illogical for that to even be considered as a possibility. More than likely, our new patient has been living a completely different lifestyle and mindset from chiropractic. There is too much of a paradigm shift that ultimately needs to occur, so meet the patient where they are at and educate them over time.

To wrap it up, their goals must be our goals. We can show them later what life could really be like with true health. However, we must stay focused on their goals in our report and then if we do lose our connection, we must reconnect with rapport and be human.

Most importantly, remember that the doctors that your new patients have seen before you likely did not seem human and didn't connect with them, or they would have stayed with that previous doctor.

Your commitment as a doctor should include this in a daily affirmation and when you feel it's just a natural, make sure you test yourself by looking at your stats honestly. The ones that got away are possibly the ones that fit in this exact picture.

Here is one of my favorite daily affirmations from <u>The Complete Works of Florence Scovel Shinn</u>:

"I have perfect work, in a perfect way. I give perfect service for perfect pay."

Chapter 8
ARE YOU LISTENING?

*"Doing your best at this moment puts
you in the best place for the next moment."*
- Oprah

Listening….that can be so…**boring**!

What if you knew that it would save your life? Or make you tons of cash? Or, actually save someone else's life? For Real.

That's different then! You'd listen to every single word, phrase, etc.!

Someone really smart said that when your mouth is open, your ears are closed and vice versa. Wow, think about it…how true!

How does this apply to a chiropractor in a busy office that doesn't really want to hear symptoms all day and has zero time to chit chat?

It applies 100% to YOU!

Paying attention is an interesting statement. The word "paying" is in there for a reason. It costs something and usually it costs time.

The next new patient is depending on your listening skills like never before. Can you imagine how they would feel if they knew what your thoughts were while they were telling you their history? Uh OH! Not good!

You can get distracted and daydream and especially when you have a new patient in front of you that is rambling. I get it. I've been there, too. You just can't stay there. There is a moment you stay there too long, and the new patient just told you something that was earth shattering and you did your usual nod or mumbled, "hmmm". Way to Go, Doc…you just lost them!

Guess who listens to your new patient when you are not around? No one. Not their kids, their spouse, their best friend. Not one single soul!

Often times, the new patient has only changed their tone with a very inconspicuous inflection. A huge clue to a listener but to someone that is distracted it will fly right past them. Pay attention. That inflection indicates some depth to the topic. It might hint at that they are shutting down and will never trust you. It may mean that they're really questioning what they're saying and maybe they feel they are not saying enough.

If you miss that they'll never stop talking!

The typical doctor nod doesn't cut it here at all! You must stay focused and stay engaged and at that last possible moment is usually when they give up the secret to unlocking their lock and snagging the diagnosis.

It could be a nonverbal cue that you missed because you were writing something down at that moment. Nonverbal cues are hard to find when you rewind the tape to listen. It's gone forever. The patient could literally be tearing up telling you something even though their voice is strong and you missed it because you were not paying attention and actually looking another direction.

There is that word again…paying. It does cost you greatly when you don't pay attention.

We probably both agree that chiropractic saves lives. When you have that new patient, pay attention. It won't **cost** you and it will **save t**hem.

Saving lives is what we do, after all, isn't it?

Chapter 9

MARKETING TRUTH #2:

SCARCITY... IS A GOOD THING

"Our typical reaction to scarcity hinders our ability to think."
— Robert B. Cialdini

One of the most important concepts that you can incorporate into your business is the concept of scarcity.

Successful businesses incorporate this concept in their marketing efforts. However, the ability to understand best practices on how to interweave scarcity into your messaging is vital so you don't suffer a crash 'n burn scenario.

First, what is scarcity in marketing? Simply put, people are more likely to take action when they know there's a chance that they will lose. It's what millennials call "FOMO" (fear of missing out) and it's a very real thing.

Remember K-Mart's *Blue Light Special* from back in the day? I remember, shopping with my mom as a kid, and we'd be in a random aisle when you'd see the flashing blue light… people would literally run over towards the neon blue light to see what the deal of the moment was all about.

Most times, those purchases were in fact impulse buys. I mean… do you really need another table runner? It didn't matter, because the psychology of feeling like you got a great deal justified the purchase in the end.

My mother loved those deals, so did the flurry of shoppers, clearly there were dopamine hits left and right. These impulse buys were emotional responses, not a logical ones. People don't often buy what they need, they buy what they want in the moment.

When a resource is scarce, it makes it more attractive in a prospect's eyes. Think about diamonds for a moment. They're a scarce resource and we all know that. Because of it, the price of diamonds are inherently high. However, when any other product is in short supply, the price often rises, along with the intimate desire to take action and purchase it. Supply and demand, basic economics.

So, you can see how scarcity is a very big driver of sales, as long as it's real scarcity and not an attempt to dupe your customers. When you try to dupe prospects into thinking that something is scarce, you end up upsetting them more than you end up fueling sales.

So, when you are launching your own promotion with hints of scarcity, make sure that it is set up the right way. If you say, "10 spots only available" be clear and honor that.

Never ever ever (ever ever) try to fool your customers, because they are no fools and the repercussions will be detrimental. Ultimately, short gains will have long term effects because your brand promise will suffer. So, use scarcity strategically and be honorable in your execution.

Chapter 10
BRING BACK THE WONDER

"Life is a 10-speed bike. Most of us have gears we never use."
– Charles Shultz

It's so awesome to watch a child experience something fun for the first time. It can be something simple, like a new object. There is utter fascination. My favorite part is observing the complete sense of WONDER displayed by the child.

Remember that, feeling...WONDER? No expectations, just being open to the experience. No labeling the experience ahead of time, instead staying in the moment and letting it unfold. Such a great feeling.

Part of the reason we love vacations, new relationships, even new purchases is that we get to experience WONDER as an adult and it feels great! We get to step back and feel something new.

You see our brains, in their infinite efficiency, pre-label and pre-categorize daily experiences for us. Ever notice that when you drive into work you may completely forget moments of the drive? That's your brain pre-categorizing the experience so that you can focus on something else.

That's problematic in practice. Especially if you've been practicing for a while. It is all too easy to look at each patient and/or their problem as something that you've seen before. It's easy to shut out the experience and focus on something else...perhaps even as that patient is right there before you!

Why do you think you get tired? Experience burn out? Get fried? Have patients quit care?

Because there is no spark. Everything seems the same. You get in a rut. You suck in that state!

Remember the first time you took a patient history? How about the feeling when you delivered your first adjustment? Was there some excitement? Ok, maybe some fear too...fair enough. However, you've been doing this long enough to throw away the fear!

Bring back the magic docs. Pause for a millisecond and look through the eyes of a child. Listen to that patient like you've never heard it before. Hang on every word, bring back the WONDER. Palpate like you've never felt a subluxation before. Feel the adjustment like it's the first time you've ever felt a bone move.

Check in and get connected throughout each shift in the office. Get enthralled and do it daily. Notice how enjoyable the day becomes. Notice how fast the time flies by.

The simplicity of being present and giving WONDER to life's experiences takes you to the top of your game.

Enjoy your success by bringing back the WONDER!

Chapter 11
CHIROPRACTIC PROSPERITY

"If not us, who? If not now, when?"
– John F. Kennedy

Prosperity in chiropractic isn't the norm.

We all see the red flags. There are offices giving away chiropractic all the time. There are offices closing constantly. There is alarming attrition within the ranks of chiropractic.

This is concerning.

It's concerning for the entire profession!

The extinction of chiropractic isn't what anyone wants (most of us anyway!). We can change our profession. We must change our profession.

Which means we must change our mindset. There's a view among many that prosperity is bad and we should be happy with what we get. I call BS!! Prosperity is Queen in my book.

Here's why…

If we have prosperity in our offices, our finances, health, families, spiritual life then we will never become extinct. Never.

When we look at history, we can see why certain things become extinct. Prosperity left the building.

We must aggressively run towards prosperity. Run Full Force towards prosperity!! It's not a game!! You must become disciplined, you must become completely committed, you must become totally confident in YOU.

Prosperity is waiting.

Prosperity is the greatest word ever. It often is associated with money, but it is the description for anything: Health, Love, Spirituality, and Mindset are some examples.

What's is your prosperity level?

Let's change that to a higher level and put extinction in the trash forever.

Chapter 12

THE PERFECT PRACTICE

"It's kinda fun to do the impossible."
– Walt Disney

What is that anyway...The Perfect Practice?? Who has a perfect practice? Is there such a thing as a perfect practice?

There is a perfect practice. It's the one you have right now!

It IS perfect....perfect for you. Look at it as if it had 10 categories. My guess is that somewhere between 6-8 categories are really good to great in your practice. Because practices are evolutionary and constantly growing and expanding, that is really pretty amazing that it's 60-80% awesome!

Can we do better?

HellaYeah!

Why do we focus on what is bad in our practice though? We have all looked at an awesome practice and told ourselves how bad things are in it.

What you think about you bring about! We have all heard that and we have all tossed that idea out when it's not convenient.

January 1st many of us will be writing down our goals, dreams, desires and plans for the next twelve months. Did you know that over 90% of those plans go out the window within four weeks? FOUR Weeks! Amazing that it can go out the window so fast!

Have you planned what your Perfect Practice looks like this year? What the Perfect Practice feels like this year? What the Perfect Practice even smells like or tastes like? You might think about doing so.

Adding several steps to your New Year's planning will make sure you are not a statistic at the end of January. In fact, you can be a rock star and have The Perfect Practice; that is if that is what you want!

Here's the list of how to plan for The Perfect Practice:

1. Define what the perfect practice is for you. It's truly dynamic and it should take some time and it should be more than just one sentence. Do what you love and make sure that the time you are committing to is something that you are 100% all in to doing. There is no half way. Put some specific time lines on it, i.e. monthly and quarterly, and you'll have a great map for what this journey will look like this year.
2. Look at the business and see what has been working and what hasn't been working. Don't skip this step, it's huge!
3. Trends. There are trends in marketing and in our businesses. Look at click funnels for example. A huge trend with big payoffs. Look at those trends and plug in what you'd like to add to your schedule, your marketing, your staff, your services, etc. There are many ways to add profits and to gain more market share.
4. Plan your time off. Rest, Relaxation, Rejuvenation. Planning this gives your brain a time out to look forward to and will create more patient retention and money that you can imagine! My bff always says that you can't keep the jet up in the air flying all the time…you have to land the jet to refuel and re-stock. I love that saying! Live by it!
5. This step is crucial for the finishing touches. Toast to the New Year as if it is already over and you've achieved all you have dreamed of and more for the year. We love doing this action step because it seals in the goals into your subconscious mind and that is the big muscle we all use to leap tall buildings. So, bring out the

best bubbly from France you can get your hands on and congratulate yourself on achieving more than you've ever imagined possible!

You are all great, incredible doctors that need to swing for the fence this year!

Put this into action, get off your bum and be the ROCKSTAR you were meant to be!!

CHEERS TO THE BEST YEAR EVER!!!

Chapter 13

MARKETING TRUTH #3:

PRICING LIKE A PRO

"Price is what you pay, value is what you get."
- Warren Buffett

All too often, when the topic of pricing comes up with our clients, we see the inevitable cringe of "I think I'm pricing too low" or "I need help with my pricing, because I'm not sure if I'm pricing right."

Have you ever heard of "the decoy effect"? It's a pricing that puts the middle-priced option very close to the highest-priced option, and has the ability to quickly propel sales of the highest-priced option as opposed to either the middle-priced option or lowest-priced option.

The sole purpose of the decoy is to effectively increase the sales of the targeted pricing option. It works by being a decoy, inducing sales of the desired option.

You've probably seen this pricing strategy at a movie theatre. That popcorn sale was a well thought out strategy in fact.

Let's just say that there are two pricing options for popcorn at a theater.

- Small popcorn is $3.00
- Large popcorn is $7.00

In this case, most people are going to go with the $3 option because of price sensitivity and that the price is far more reasonable. It makes sense, right? Why spend $7 on a large popcorn when you can get a small popcorn for $3. That's more than double the price for the large from the small-sized popcorn. In this case, most people are going to opt for the less expensive option because it just makes more sense.

But what happens when you make a small addition by adding the decoy? What if you add a third option and price it at $6.50? This decoy changes the game so that the buyer's attention is focused on the large option because it's a better value.

- Small popcorn is $3.00
- Medium popcorn (decoy) is $6.50
- Large popcorn is $7.00

So, when you are pricing your own services, make sure to offer three distinct offerings and position a mid-tier as the decoy. It's still a win if someone purchases, but they are statistically more inclined to choose the higher option because of the additional value at an incremental cost.

Boom!

Chapter 14

DO YOU TESLA?

"It is not your customer's job to remember you. It is your obligation and responsibility to make sure they don't have the chance to forget you."
– Patricia Fripp

You have to respect Elon Musk. Why? Consider this: his buyers are rabidly plunking down 50k deposits for the upcoming Tesla Roadster. (If you want to be in the first 1000, it's 250k). No big deal right? Look further...

His buyers have no hard delivery date. In fact, they will not receive their prized vehicle until around 2020!!!

Now that takes GUTS and CONVICTION to close a deal and demand that your buyer wait three YEARS for a product that he or she has never touched, felt, or driven. No instant gratification: money upfront and delayed celebration.

There is this not so little phenomenon call buyer's remorse. And BUYERS REMORSE = DIVORCE. Buyer's remorse is a POWERFUL emotion. That's your patient that converts to care and then stays for 1-5 visits and splits.

Musk develops buyer's elation...sustained excitement that stays the course of time. BUYER'S ELATION = CELEBRATION. Tesla buyers feel extraordinarily lucky to be on the delivery list to receive the world's fastest production car--no matter how long it takes. How many of your patients have buyer's elation? How many celebrate each visit and complete their care plan, no matter how long it takes? How many have enough sustained buyer's elation to celebrate converting to your maintenance care?

Are you a one hit wonder or are you filling your practice with acres of diamonds? Do you cultivate patients that are looking for a single $45 adjustment or investing in a lifetime of wellness?

How do you create buyer's elation? It's not a motion study. It's not a life effect. In fact, it's not what you think at all. There are several secrets to buyer's elation, and one of them is DYNAMIC DRIVERS: a patient focused, non-scripted conversation that evolves from day one and continues throughout care. It is congruency throughout the care with WHY the patient bought in the first place. It is not TICing them to death. It is not life-effecting them into submission. It is the art of connecting the dots for your patient to consistently built excitement and RELEVANCE for something they won't live without: YOUR CARE.

When you understand how to create buyer's elation and use dynamic drivers...then you too can Tesla.

Ready to learn more? Let's keep the conversation going!

Chapter 15
DON'T BE AN ISLAND

*"I have insecurities of course,
but I don't hang out with anyone that points them out."*
- Adele

Chiropractors take hits from all sides. Being in practice can be immensely satisfying, yet it is not all lollipops and unicorns. You are expected to wear many hats: Doctor, employer, risk management officer, visionary, CEO, etc. And you must deal with the ups and downs of each responsibility and the associated pitfalls and criticisms.

We are small businesses that are often expected by the public to compare to large medical corporations with endless resources at their fingertips. We are the little guys in a sea of big fish.

You cannot exist as an island. It takes too much energy. Find your community of like-minded people within chiropractic and leverage resources. Like cyclists in a peloton, you increase efficiency and conserve energy for a more positive outcome.

If you are a ten minute per mile runner that desires to improve, would it help you to run with fifteen-minute mile runners? Not likely. How about 4-minute milers? Again, not likely as you would be immensely frustrated. (The four-minute milers would however train your headspace that a four-minute mile is indeed possible). The answer is that you would most likely improve running with runners that were a notch above you in their abilities. Like say a group of eight to nine-minute mile runners. And an even better scenario is various groups of defined levels within a larger community that you could grow and ascend levels with at your own pace as you improve.

Select your chiropractic community carefully. Is the glass half full or half empty? Are you uplifted by your peeps or drained? Are you reinventing wheels, or do you have mentoring and visionary leadership?

And speaking of leadership, nobody is perfect. However, are those that you look up to honest? Truthful? Ethical? Do they raise the standard in you and chiropractic? And how much effort have you put into vetting your experts?

Years ago, as a chiropractic student, I visited many chiropractic offices that were gracious enough to allow me to shadow their doctors. It was a phenomenal experience. I will never forget when I shadowed an associate doctor that worked in the clinic of a hugely prominent chiropractic coach (who still coaches to this day). It was perfectly acceptable in their office to show the films of two different patients as a "before" and "after" example of care. The problem was that patients were led to believe that the films represented a single patient that improved with care!

Chiropractic is such a great and honorable profession, we don't need to exaggerate our claims or falsify facts. We need to align ourselves with everything and everyone that bring out the greatness of chiropractic.

Chapter 16
BEING CERTAIN

"Opportunity is missed by most people because it's dressed in overalls and looks like work."
—Thomas Jefferson

Being certain about: what you're doing, saying, even about who you are. That's the key, right? Easy to say but hard to act on.

The most successful people really seem to have this attribute. They "seem" to have it…they make sure you think they have it. But do they really? You have heard "fake it till you make it", right?

Here's the thing, no one is born being certain. Not ONE person. As a Doctor in a professional setting you must be more certain than EVER!!

How do you get there though? The answer is a short one. It takes **time** and **practice.**

Yes. Time and practice is how it's done.

The most incredible, beautiful things took time to occur and came with lots and lots of practice.

Look at how long it took "overnight sensations" like, Vince Gill, Dolly Parton, U2, Bruce Springsteen, Bob Dylan, to make it! I could keep going, too. It took years!

You must be so committed that every single day you do these three things to make this happen.

Conceptualize.

Creating the concept or idea is what conceptualize means.

Conceptualize the idea of what you'd like life, your practice, etc., to be. What you want *in* your life and what you want to *happen*. In specific order and detail. Make sure you know every single piece of the puzzle. This is where you design your dreams. All of them by the way, not just some of your dreams.

Visualize.

Paint the actual picture in your mind of what you've created in your mind as success. What does it look like, what does it feel like, what does it even smell like? Bring this up in your mind and visualize it as if it were already happening and you can see yourself in the picture. It's a beautiful, perfect image! Etch it into your brain to bring up on a daily basis and even multiple times a day! Meditate with commitment and conviction!

Actualize.

The actualize step is exactly what it says it is...it is an **action** step. This is a physical boots on the ground movement that you do on the daily with relentless energy and commitment. You can't let up and ease through this step because this step is the one that brings the beautiful images you have in your mind into reality and across the finish line for you to enjoy and relish in! You can actually live your dream from this point on!

You are the inventor, photographer and podium finisher of your dreams! You can go through any list of wants that you have, put these three steps into a habit and you will have anything you want.

Understand that at first you'll need to practice these steps intentionally. Over time when you've performed these steps on a consistent basis, you will get better and better. It will become a habit!

You must realize deep in your heart that you want it so bad that nothing will stop you, that you deserve it, the world needs you to be the baller you were designed to be, and life is much better on this level. Period.

You must embrace this "time and practice" rule to be **Certain.**

Embrace it Now.

Chapter 17

CATCH SUCCESS

*"There is one thing I know.
Never in history has panic solved anything."*
-Steven Soderbergh

Do you have standard operating procedures (SOPs)? Are they written down? If a new employee came into the practice tomorrow, how long would it take to bring them up to speed? Would you and/or the new employee become frustrated with each other due to lack of progress?

Every practice needs defined systems and procedures. When an office is running at peak, there is no time to decide "who's on first base". Your systems and procedures allow for your office to run like a Swiss clock and to accept expansion without pain. During "happy hour" when your office is at its busiest, can you take in an unexpected new patient seamlessly and without every other patient in the building suffering? If opportunity knocks, will you and your team see it and capitalize on it? Or will you get lost in the efforts of inefficiency and turn opportunity away?

SOPs define expectations of employees and allow for reflection and growth in a practice. Roles are defined and duties expressed. Standards are created and processes are plotted for efficiency. A baseline is visualized and a culture borne.

What is the culture of your office? One of confusion, negativity and frustration? Or one of growth, possibility and positivity?

Do your employees have defined roles and know what is expected of them? (And are they the right person for their particular position? More on that later.)

A great way to begin to formulate standard operating procedures for your practice is to do an exercise that we like to call "Catch Success".

Here's what you need to Catch Success:

Bring a stuffed doll into your next staff meeting. You are going to begin by mapping the journey of a new patient through your office during their first visit. Have the staff sit in a circle with one person scribing the journey. Throw the doll to whomever greets your new patient at the front desk and write down their duties, like greet the new patient, give them their paperwork to fill out, copy or scan their ID and insurance card, etc. Next, throw the doll to whomever takes the new patient back and write down the duties associated with that task, like greet the new patient and escort the patient to the consultation room, bring the paperwork for the doctor, make sure that the doctor has the appropriate consultation and exam forms, etc. Continue to throw the doll to each person associated with every aspect of the new patient's first visit and document the duties for each step in the patient journey.

Try not to "drop the doll" because essentially, that's where you're letting your new patient down in their initial experience in your office!

After you have completed the first visit, map out the journey for the second visit, regular office visits, re-exam visits, etc.

If you perform this exercise carefully and accurately, you will have a great start on formulating your standard operating procedures. From there you can add details and refine expectations.

You will add structure and order to your practice so that you don't have "who's on first?" moments in your office. You will also have a game plan for new employees to learn from.

Go ahead doc, Catch *YOUR* Success!

Chapter 18
MARKETING TRUTH #4: MESSAGING MATTERS

"Your words do not return void"
- Florence Scovell-Schinn

Ever wonder if your brand messaging is hitting the mark with your customers/patients?

Think about your favorite brands? There's a strong probability that you connected with the brand because of a connection you feel with that brand.

You know how Volvo is all about *safety?* The company's ethos is all centered around their core sentiment of safety.

Sure, big brands have big brand budgets, but the goal of any business is to be ONE thing in the mind of your customers. Just one. If you can't narrow it down to one, you've lost.

Do your customers know you for one thing? If not, what do you want to be known for? And, if you aren't sure, the next question is: how do YOU make your brand messaging strong?

Here are some quick tips:

Keep it simple

While we want to be all things to all people, we have to pick a lane and stay in it.

What is the ONE thing your company can do better than any competitor?

If you aren't sure, ask your current customers. Send out a survey, ask them when they are in your office. Ask them as they are leaving. Ask them.

You'll start to identify common words and adjectives that you probably weren't aware of; there's power in asking your customers.

Now highlight the ONE thing.

What's the rational value? For example in Volvo's case: car

What's the emotional value of what you offer? *Volvo makes cars that are safe for my family.*

Notice how the connection between the rational value and emotional value in essence connects the head to the heart. You have to have both in order to make an emotional connection with your customers.

Make sure your messaging is always relevant to your customer

In other words, make sure that your ideal customer wants what you have.

Ultimately, the goal is to capture precious mindshare in your customer's mind... that's how customer loyalty is built over time.

Remember that more repeat customers equals more profits.

Chapter 19
BUST A RUT

"The most unprofitable item ever manufactured is an excuse."
– John Mason

Are you stuck? Can't get more new patients? Stuck at the same volume? Same conversion rate? Practice stats looking flat, or trending downward?

We've all been there. The truth is that you have to change something. And the quicker you make the change(s), the sooner your stress level and mood improve. After all, the definition of insanity is doing the same thing over and over and expecting a different result.

Two key components to success are adaptability and flexibility. Funny thing- these two traits are the first to leave when you get set in your ineffective ways. You must train your brain and physiology your entire life to remain adaptable and flexible. In order to be adaptable and flexible, you must embrace change.

First, start change with yourself. Do something different. Change your physiology and brain processes. For example, drive a different way to or from work. Start the day with a cold shower. Put your pants on using the other leg first. Brush your teeth starting with the other side of your mouth. As silly as these changes in habits seem, they create a flexible brain that keeps learning.

In order to reach the next level, you must remain flexible and force yourself out of your comfort zone and habits. It is in the new zone that you can expand. This is where true growth occurs.

Ultimately you may have to also change several things, such as office systems and processes in order to get out of a rut. And we always want to change something or someone else other than ourselves. However, as a leader you must change within first so that your team may follow.

You see, practices are mirror images of ourselves. If your intention is to change your practice you must first be willing to change yourself. Change your mental state. Change your physiology.

The overwhelming majority of the tasks necessary to be successful involve creating change, adapting new structure and tapping into wonder. The sooner that you embrace change, the sooner you move up the ladder of personal success and live in the presence of peace, health and freedom.

So, start with the small steps like driving home from work a different way. Celebrate your new-found mental flexibility and adaptability. Then build on it. You are on your way to the path of your dreams once you commit to that first small step. Stay the course and go for it!

Chapter 20

THE ADJUSTMENT IS #1!!

"People don't buy what you do; they buy why you do it. And what you do simply proves what you believe."
– Simon Sinek

Makes sense, right? If that makes sense to you, we are on the same page. However, from what I can tell, many DC's have forgotten that Golden Rule.

Here's why I say they may have forgotten that concept. I have seen many, many posts on private Facebook pages with questions stating, "what do I do if xx happens.." and the doctor will have a laundry list of items they have tried and nothing is listed about the adjustment. Did they assume that we knew the adjustment was part of it or did they leave it off of the list? Occasionally another doctor will add "adjustment" in the thread with a single question mark like maybe that was being overlooked but no one wanted to mention that fact.

There are tons of students that don't know that the adjustment is the end all be all. Many students want to study approaches other than chiropractic for patients or they will refer the patient to an allopath for future care because the patient still has leg pain after 6 chiropractic visits. You and I both know that chiropractic can be amazing for these patients but so many doctors aren't giving it a second thought and we also know that there's more to that story and we will get down to the nitty gritty on that subject later.

The adjustment is #1!

Your vision of your successful practice didn't consist of referring a large majority of your patients to the medical doctor or anywhere else, unless clinically necessary, I am sure.

Listen to what you tell your patients on a daily basis. For that matter, what you told them in the report of findings the day they accepted care from you. You can include the statement, "The adjustment is the #1 thing you'll receive here to correct your problem". If you love and adore chiropractic that will be an easy thing to include in your report of findings. The adjustment isn't the treatment; the care plan is the treatment, by the way. You don't ever need to minimize the adjustment.

When we minimize the adjustment, it is very confusing to the patient. You may tell them all about other services in your office and never mention that the adjustment is what the secret is to the sauce. Why would you ever do that and expect the patient to return, pay and refer? It's a sure thing, they won't do any such thing unless they see you as unique. Confused patients don't buy anything either. The Adjustment is #1!

You are the most unique doctor on the planet in that you can take a sick, dis-eased, diseased patient and guide them to health and wellness. This is your unique selling point. You need to know it, own it and share it on the daily with your patients. Then they will see you as the only solution in town and drive past medical doctors, hospitals and even other chiropractors to get to you.

A health map, a plan of attack for their diagnosis is the way to go and the adjustment should be delivering the megaton correction for your patient and they should be able to recite that back to you after visit 2. It's good to have the patient repeat what you told them. You have to let them know why they bought everything you said and the retention in your office will skyrocket. The Adjustment is #1!

Make it crystal clear to the patient that they have made the right decision because you have the answers they've been looking for. They were right to step into your place of healing because that unique solution, the one no one else has offered them, is right in front of them.

Think about how you feel about the adjustment. Is it the key to all things health and wellness related? Yes! Of course it is, and as it should be, so offer it to the patient as a unique solution that stands alone in its oneness. The Adjustment is #1!

Here's what is possibly happening; we discount our gift. Our adjustment is our gift, like a great singing voice or the ability to paint, it is our healing gift. We use it so much that we begin to discount it and think that other things will be necessary to heal a person. Truly if we all had to pick one thing to heal us, most of us would pick an adjustment bar none! When we add other things, we can do so without discounting the adjustment. We can add nutrition, essential oils, therapies, rehab, etc. and still make the adjustment number ONE. We do this by calling it the number one thing we do. Period.

The Adjustment is #1!

Chapter 21
LOOKING FOR THE NEXT SHINEY OBJECT

"Innovation distinguishes between a leader and a follower."
– Steve Jobs

There are countless doctors looking for the next great thing to turn their practice around. Are you running from one "shiny object" to another looking for answers, or at least the next magic bullet?

Success comes from effort and a series of great decisions. It also comes from knowing when to stay the course and when to cut bait. Jumping from one influence to the next, looking for instant success rarely pays off. You must be honest with yourself and do the work.

Find successful mentors that have long records of success and honesty. You can't buy integrity, you foster it from within and accept nothing less. You can't buy respect either, you earn that. Be careful of who and what you look up to.

Shiny objects are just that, shiny objects with no long-term core value. Quit running after them, wasting your precious time and money. There are plenty of people lining up to take your money. Get past the fluff and strive for substance.

Instead, look past the packaging and start asking the hard questions. Will this sustain me long-term? Does this resonate with my core values and inspire me to take measurable action steps? Does the leadership excite me to do the work necessary to get to the next level? Is there integrity involved?

The road to success is paved with good intentions and false promises. Develop great BS filters in your ears to identify the hyperbole and educated eyes to spot the smoke and mirrors. And listen to your heart and that small (always correct) voice in your head, for that is your true north.

There are so many voices in Chiropractic today – practically yelling, screaming and jumping up and down to get their messages across, to build their audiences and sell their products. And then there's the quiet voice whose message is so powerful when it drops that chaos halts to listen.

You see, our profession has essentially three types of "experts" today:

1.   **Reporters**: those that report or assimilate material or data written by others inside or outside of our profession and adapt it to their program,
2.   **Repeaters**: those that simply repeat basically the same material over and over again that was conceived or written by other DCs, and
3.   **Innovators**: those that move the profession forward by thinking outside of the box and providing real, sustainable, and successful answers to doctors in the field.

You know who the reporters and repeaters are. We all do. They're good people, using the tools they have, to help get you to where they can...which is only so far. Innovators are another story, they're a rare find. They lift you to go beyond what you know is yet possible.

Steve Jobs once said that it was pointless to ask a focus group what they wanted because they don't have any idea of what is possible. An innovator is so out of the box in their thinking that they see solutions that you do not yet see. Come learn from innovators and learn solutions that you do not yet know exist for your health, peace, and freedom.

Chapter 22
SUPERLATIVE CERTIFIED

"It is entirely possible that behind the perception of our senses, worlds are hidden of which we are unaware."
– Albert Einstein

Recently, Darci and I welcomed Rolex numbers 3, 4 and 5 into our household: in the form of Daytona, Yachtmaster and Air King.

Every new Rolex has a green medallion attached by a ribbon to it that says "Superlative Certified."

Superlative Certified, what an interesting statement. It actually refers to the fact that the watch has gone through a series of tests in Rolex's own laboratory, by their own internal standards, and is now labeled as a superlative chronometer.

Think about it, Superlative Certified....

Rolex has planted the seed by making that statement upfront. They have set themselves apart. And by virtue of the term they've coined, Rolex has essentially told its buyer that superlatives are synonymous with Rolex.

In other words...any good words or feelings associated with your Rolex are by design, EXPECT them! Brilliant and beautiful marketing. We call it THE POSITIVE PLANT.

A huge part of successful sales is PERCEPTION. Does your marketing set you and your chiropractic clinic apart by creating your own standard? And, do you POSITIVE PLANT the perception of a premier experience for your buyer? By the way, use caution and be mindful and creative: you have a state board.

Getting back to the lessons of Rolex, they deliver on the experience. The watches are of the highest quality and the buyer's experience is second to none. Once again, by design.

You see, Rolex controls everything it can to make sure that their buyer's experience is pristine. They dictate the design of the storefront, floor space and displays for each of their dealers.

Calculated details. Rolex refuses to take a back seat to any of its competitors. They build on their POSITIVE PLANT and refuse to let their buyers have a PERCEPTUAL LET DOWN.

How many times have you done great marketing, only to have your new patient encounter a PERCEPTUAL LET DOWN when their initial experience in your office did not match their expectations? In other words, your marketing was way better than the delivery in your office for the new patient. And your previously excited new patient says "Bye Felicia." How calculated are you in the design of your sale?

Every step of your BUYER'S JOURNEY must create CONGRUENT CONTEXT. What does that mean? Each step of the new patient's journey from awareness to buying must be congruent with your initial message...the POSITIVE PLANT!

One last thought...there are a million ways to create a POSITIVE PLANT in your BUYER'S JOURNEY, and you should have several. Study Rolex carefully, theirs are carefully planted in the sales cycle.

When you change the way you look at things, the things you look at change. Now there's money!

Chapter 23

MARKETING TRUTH #5:

MARKETING THAT WENT OUT WITH THE MULLET

"Marketing is like sex, everyone thinks they're good at it"
- Steve Tobak

When we were discussing the nuances of the marketing, Dr. Jeri coined a very clever phrase, *"Let's talk about the kind of Marketing That Went Out With the Mullet."* After hearty laughter and paying homage to Billy Ray Cyrus, we discussed the difference between marketing that engages and marketing that is just noise.

1989 called and they want their crappy marketing back! What does that mean? It means that as you take an honest look at your marketing and if you have a "push" approach, it's just noise. Even worse, chances are nobody's listening. And that means you're just wasting your time. Of course, frustration surfaces and you start to wonder if this marketing thing is really worth doing for your business.

I remember giving a presentation and one of the attendees came up to me and said, "thank you for making this all sound so simple. I avoid marketing like the plague! In fact, dare I say I'd rather get a root canal then to think about marketing in my business."

I invite you to take a pulse check on the marketing you've been doing and assess whether it's been a push fest.

Push marketing is a promotional strategy where businesses attempt to grab attention of prospective customers. The term push stems from the idea that business owners are attempting to push their products or services.

Common tactics include "come on in for an x-ray and adjustment, we just got a new supersonic x-ray machine with a hooby-dooby feature and more features". People do not buy features, people buy transformation. Think about "WIIFM" (what's in it for me), it's the only radio station that matters.

Pull marketing, on the other hand, takes the opposite approach. The goal of pull marketing is to get the customers to come to you, hence the term pull. I like to refer to it as "attraction." As the author Simon Sinek so eloquently put it, *"People don't buy what you do or how you do it, they buy WHY you do what you do."*

Start with more storytelling and transformation sharing. Help your prospective customers see the world through the eyes of the person who has already had the transformation. Its why public reviews work so well. We appreciate third party endorsements. It's why I pull out my phone really quick to check Yelp whenever I'm in a different city and are looking to see what the reviews say before trying a new restaurant.

Attract people into your world by sharing more of the transformation. Better yet, if you can capture your customers words on video, that's a bigger win than just a written testimonial.

And, promise us no more "hooby dooby" highlighted push marketing. And just like the mullet, it does not work.

To receive complementary resources to this book including videos, downloads, audios that will support your practice, we invite you to visit:

www.prosperityprinciplesbook.com/resources

This dynamic page will continue to provide updates that are relevant and actionable for you.

Chapter 24
WHY? NO REALLY...WHY?

"In order to be irreplaceable, one must always be different."
– Coco Chanel

Why would someone come into your office?

No kidding, WHY?

Have you ever asked yourself that question? If you haven't yet, you should have. There are a zillion other chiropractors out there for the public to choose from. So WHY should they choose you?

So few chiropractors can actually answer this question.

Patients buy YOU and the patient experience that YOU deliver in YOUR office. Plain and simple. What is unique about you and your office? What sets you apart in the market and what do you deliver that they can't and won't live without?

Before you spent a lot of time and energy on marketing, how about spending some time defining who you are? That's step one. From there you can better target your marketing efforts. It is remarkable how few doctors take this step. Great marketing exploits your uniqueness, and your strengths in the marketplace.

Universally, chiropractors want success and freedom. You gain both my becoming indispensable as a doctor, a boss and a business. What is your niche? WHY would anyone seek your services or work for you?

GET REAL. We all have strengths and niches. Done properly, we are not competing against each other. Realistically, how could we be since chiropractic occupies such a small percentage of the total healthcare market? Chiropractic as a whole would be better off if we each defined ourselves and targeted our marketing correctly to draw our own unique tribe of new patients that become our raving fans.

The art is to draw "your crowd". You must know who and what you are to segment your target markets correctly.

Food for thought. We all know that doctor that people come from all over the earth to see and don't mind waiting for. The one that doesn't work tons and tons of hours, goes on vacation lots and has patients and staff that can't live without them. Do your homework correctly and you can be THAT DOCTOR.

Start by taking pen to paper. Define who and what you are, and WHY someone would choose your office and YOU for their care?

Chapter 25
FAILURE TO PLAN, PLANNING TO FAIL

"The future belongs to those who believe in the beauty of their dreams."
– Eleanor Roosevelt

Imagine running across a blind-folded archer, with bow and arrow at the ready, aimlessly pointing at an unseen target and expecting to hit it? Crazy, huh?

Yet so many chiropractors exhibit the same behavior in their lives and practices. All hat, no cattle. Big dreams, no plan for how to get there.

What are your goals and objectives? Where will you be at in life and practice in 1, 5, 10 and 20 years from now? What will your life look and feel like?

How will you measure your progress? When will you decide if course corrections are necessary? How big is your vision?

Get pen to paper and write it down. Create your plan, your road map. Take the blindfold off and give the archer inside of you a target to hit!

Without a plan, fruition is unlikely for your dreams and goals. Do you want to be that person looking back years from now with remorseful thoughts of shoulda, woulda, coulda and unmet dreams? Or do you desire to meet your dreams and create larger ones?

Nobody is responsible for your success but you. It reminds me of the signs we have for our patients on all of the mirrors in our office: "This is the person responsible for your health." Sometimes we just need a reminder!

The good news is that you are fully capable of creating your own success, by your own terms. And it all starts with planning!

Chapter 26
LEVERAGING DISAPPOINTMENTS

"Winning is fun…sure. But winning is not the point. Wanting to win is the point. Not giving up is the point. Never letting up is the point. Never being satisfied with what you've done is the point."
– Pat Summitt

In Life and in practice we often run into events that don't meet our expectations.

Why? Why does this happen and why does it happen to us over and over are important questions.

Lessons need to be learned is the number one reason I think it happens. The reason I say that is because we often end up in a movie that's a rerun. If you think about it, you've been shown that lesson more than once. Why do we have to watch another rerun? Because we didn't learn the complete lesson. It's not unusual for us to have the same repeat lessons because we skip some of the main parts. Maybe human nature sneaks in! By the third or fourth rerun we realize that we have seen this before and NOW we got that lesson down!

It's not funny but sometimes you have to laugh that we humans are so predictable!

Another reason that we experience certain disappointments is because it could be that we need a good kick of momentum. A swift hiney kick can sure give us momentum and energy to "show them!" It's true that you need motivation to get moving towards a goal. Sometimes you need someone to make you mad so that you drop the nice person facade and move into BTW (balls to wall) mode. When you get mad enough, this is when oftentimes, your best work comes forward.

You can be easy going, nice, which can equal COMPLACENT!! YUK.

You can Not be interested in rolling over. Ever. You've heard "Don't get mad, Get Even!" It seems like that fits really well here in this situation. The bottom line is that we get hung up on whether or not someone likes us. Wayne Dyer said it best: They aren't really thinking about you all that much! That's so awesome and so perfect!! Why do we humans get high centered on the "I hope they like me" theory?

You can talk about confidence and self-esteem here all you like but there's more to it. When the right person gets beat down enough, and a few other bad things happen to them, they can sometimes buy into the negative train of thought and they can convince themselves that they have a self-worth issue. It happens all the time. If that didn't happen, all doctors would get along, make money, never go out of business, and most negative emotions would never stick to you like they currently tend to.

Buying into the fact that you're awesome is integral to your success. You know it's absolutely crucial. You are fierce. You're one of a kind. This is your story; write it how you like. The pen is in your hand and you get to write the story how you'd like it to be. Then before you know it, you've drafted exactly how it turns out.

What you think and focus on is what you get. You've heard that a million times: If you think it's the perfect storm for negativity, then it IS! If you think it's the perfect moment for success and you can't be stopped, then you're right! You are the one with your foot on the gas or the brake. It's a decision, YOUR decision to make.

It seems simple and it can be simple. When you are stuck is when you really convince yourself that it's complicated. Often the decision is the hardest part. Once your mind is made up, the work part can actually be easy. The conscious mind can be a gatekeeper and it can slow down the subconscious achiever. If you open the gate for your subconscious mind, there truly is no limit to your success. So why limit yourself?

Use the disappointments as a springboard and let them give you momentum, energy, and the fight mentality that you need to achieve the next goal.

Take the energy you've spent being mad and direct it into getting ahead. That is powerful energy and you need to use it to get ahead of the competition!

You can change your mind and make the decision to "Win" just as easily as sitting there and it'll be more fun and more productive. Once you have a win and catch even more momentum, chances are that you'll win again!! Then it's a whole new ballgame!

Learn the lessons life gives you and use them to your advantage, and then take that energy and pour that fuel into your next project!! Success is yours!!

Chapter 27

COVET YOUR LICENSE AND STAY OUT OF JAIL

"In the middle of every difficulty lies opportunity."
– Albert Einstein

It is doubtful that a doctor embroiled in a malpractice case or board complaint case set out on a given day to get themselves into trouble. Sure, there will always be cases of intentional acts of moral turpitude, as there are always rotten eggs and bad apples. However, the majority of doctors in these situations make a series of poor and/or ill-informed decisions to get to that place of trouble.

The days are gone for "the dog ate my homework". You are a licensed professional that is expected to behave like one. After all, the public you serve are entrusting you with their lives'.

Today's practice environment requires you to stay abreast of coding, compliance, HIPAA, Medicare, OIG and other regulatory requirements at an unprecedented level. And, the landscape is ever changing regarding these regulations.

One of your best investments is an onsite visit and audit from a coding and compliance expert. It is always better to be more informed than less informed. Educate yourself and take care of deficiencies before they become problems. Follow that up with regular scheduled training. The upside of your investment is that you will sleep well at night!

Alternatively, there are also web-based trainings and webinars to bring you up to speed. While you will not have eyes on your files, as in a pro-active audit with an expert, it is likely that you will learn a ton to shore up your record keeping and files. Many malpractice carriers have resources to help train you as well.

So, perhaps you don't want to spend the cash for an onsite visit or online training? Then it's best to ask yourself a few questions: What are you doing annually and regularly to self-audit? How well are your staff trained to carry out procedures that protect your license? How do you know that you are compliant? If an auditor arrived at your office tomorrow, what would you do and what would your level of concern be? How well are you prepared?

How well can you answer these critical questions? Your license equals your ability to practice and earn an income. Are you taking your license for granted or protecting it?

Chapter 28
TECHNIQUE

"The expectations of life depend upon diligence; the mechanic that would perfect his work must first sharpen his tools."
- Confucius

So many docs get into discussions about which technique is the best one in chiropractic. The truth of the matter is that all techniques have their awesome attributes, but it is really a personal preference. The best technique you should do for your patients is the one you are the very best at performing and the one that gets your patients the best results. It is as simple as that, I promise.

With that said there are some serious caveats.

It must be a valid technique and one that you are very adept at performing.

Looking at really successful offices, there is usually one main technique that is practiced and some back up techniques, if you will. The main technique is used on most patients and the backup techniques are used when what you do doesn't work or the patient doesn't respond like you'd want them to respond.

You must have a great, easy to understand explanation of your technique down pat. This comes in super handy when you are explaining to the patient what the #1 thing (the chiropractic adjustment) will be that you do to correct their problem(s) and you will sound professional and time will be saved because it will prevent endless questions.

Your technique must incorporate checks and balances so that the you and the patient can know a pre-adjustment status and a post adjustment status. This is a great way to manage the patient and also very helpful for the doctor.

Most patients have no idea what procedures you are doing when they are on the table, so you need to let them know how they were before and after the adjustment. We take a show and tell approach with our patients. For example: we often say quite loudly, "There

115

it is, we found it!" during palpation of a tender area when the patient is prone so that they understand that we are looking for the problem, finding the problem and correcting the problem. To the patient that is everything! You should have many pre and post checks in your arsenal to show and tell your patient the changes to their health with the adjustment.

The pre and post checks must be speedy and efficient. Time is the commodity that you are operating in so you must make each second count. If palpation is your favorite pre and post check, that is great. Have the patient lying prone so that when you get to them it is an efficient scan and you are adjusting them in no time.

If you study your favorite technique you will find that most have great pre and post checkups and they are very time efficient. Our society is fast paced today, most patients are not on your table for a social visit. They have places to go and things to get done in their day. The idea of spending 15 minutes with a patient on the table is not going to be super helpful to either one of you. It takes very little time to deliver an awesome adjustment and even less to do pre and post checkups.

This doesn't include the tricky patient or new trauma type patient. Even on those patients we have a set way to approach those folks with an appropriate, efficient exam and follow up procedures. These patients don't make up your entire day though, but you must have a protocol in place for them.

It is a must that you learn new information every single year. Even if it is one thing that you add to your list of tools in your tool belt, you must keep learning. Patients have different problems all the time so it's great when you can be their source for answers. It won't be long that you'll have a favorite protocol for all situations. It may be straight forward problems like frozen shoulder, TMJD, headaches, all the way to complicated, tough problems like degenerative spondys with leg pain. Don't let the patient go down the street because you were too lazy and stayed home from a weekend seminar that would've made all the difference to them.

Patients are so much easier to manage and will refer more often when you have your technique down to a science. The patient truly looks at you as their hero/shero when you operate like that. You are precise, not guessing, not chasing symptoms, confident, even if your experience isn't there yet, they will believe in you with all they have and fill up your office with acres and acres of diamonds.

You must always relate the problem back to the chiropractic subluxation diagnosis. That is why they came to you because you have the solution for that problem that no one else has. Every day connect the subluxation to their problem and say it to the patient and they will be your biggest cheerleader ever. No one figured out what was wrong with them but you, and no one cared to do that for them either. If your patients are telling you that you are a miracle worker (which they should be) that is the reason why. That is one of the many reasons' chiropractic is so great!

To recap, your patients need you to be the best most efficient doctor that they have ever met. They are putting their trust in you and you must rise to the occasion. You must have the technique down solid and you must assess the patient daily. You must be time sensitive. Decide if what you are doing is exactly what they need that day or is it something else entirely. Develop a standard of care for your office and never waiver. Be committed to that level of care and nothing less and your office will be filled with a deep, loyal group of beautiful healthy fans. There will be no competition: you are their Doctor, their hero and their answer.

Chapter 29

MARKETING TRUTH #6:

THE THREE WAYS TO GROW YOUR BUSINESS

"Do what you do so well that they will want to see it again and tell their friends"
- Walt Disney

Did you know that there is truly only three ways to grow your business? We like simple and simple is what wins the business game. This was one of the best moments... to realize that by focusing on just three concepts, you can grow your business sustainably.

The first way to grow your business is to focus on "getting more customers." In essence, it's what most businesses focus on, "how to get more customers," "where do I find more customers?" Most marketing service providers promote customer acquisition because that's what most business owners focus on.

As mentioned in other marketing sections here in this book, you know that it's more strategic to focus on attraction that connects, not "getting new customers". You want to fish where the fish are, not hunt. Hunting is pushing and forcing. Fishing is where you use bait, that is relevant, to attract the right fish. The exact fish that you are looking for. What bait do you use? The bait that is timely and relevant to the fish.

The second way to grow your business is to tap into your current base and sell them more. In the internet marketing world, this is known as the "ascension ladder." Most small business owners have a one and done selling approach where they are at the mercy of waiting for new customers, instead of creating repeat customers. Within your business, do you have more than just one thing to sell? Ask yourself, "what else can I offer them? What's next for my customer?" Will all your customers purchase again? No. But there will be a percentage that do, and that adds to the bottom line significantly because you have already acquired that customer.

The third way to grow your business is to focus on recurring revenue. What can you sell your customers where you are paid again and again? Perhaps a membership? A subscription? The goal is to have your customers purchase every month. Look at your offerings and see where you can incorporate a recurring revenue model. This is a golden opportunity to increase the (LTV) lifetime value of your customers.

Chapter 30

INITIATE INTENTION

"Greatness is not a function of circumstance. Greatness it turns out, is largely a matter of conscious choice."
– Jim Collins

Want to stay in integrity with yourself? Then set your intention for everything that you do.

Want to be the best doctor to your patients? Simple. Every single time you lay your hands on them, set your intention to heal them. Yeah, you have to mentally check in with yourself versus blabbing to the patient as you adjust on autopilot. Don't kid yourself, patients know the difference.

Want the secret to the practice of your dreams? Set your intention and map your journey to success. You see, super great things in life rarely happen without intention and planning.

Ready to map the day? Great! First thing when you wake, put your phone down. Please put that damn thing down. It sucks the life out of you. Instead, start your day with INTENTION.

Close your eyes and visualize your perfect day. New patients calling and coming into your office, LOTS of them! Your staff handling everything seamlessly. Visualize all the patients streaming into your office happily. Visualize your fantastic adjustments for your patients. Listen to your conversations. Hear their satisfaction and referral language. See the successful outcome to any stressor that you may have to deal with. Feel your boundless energy and goodwill.

Now get up and GO GET IT!

Everything you do and every project you touch must be met with INTENTION. You must chart the course and seed the path to success.

Have you looked at your relationship with your significant other? Are you intending to LOVE and CHERISH that person until your last breath? What are you doing to make that happen? Setting intentions allows you to appreciate the gifts in your life and to live it. Start with those that you love most. Do your spouse and kids feel your intention towards them? If not, fix that NOW.

By the way, intend to have FUN and ENJOY the journey. In your down time, intend to relax and enjoy the fruits of life. It's ok to put your feet up and enjoy the view from the TOP!

Chapter 31

IF YOU WEAR OUT YOUR BODY, WHERE ARE YOU GOING TO LIVE?

"How do you build up your bank account? By putting something in it every day. Your health account is no different. What I do today, I am wearing tomorrow. If I put inferior foods in my body today, I'm going to be inferior tomorrow, it's that simple."
– *Jack Lalanne*

How many times do chiropractors give their patients advice that the doctor does not follow themselves? Are you congruent in practice, or are you a contradiction? Your patients figure that out by the way.

Pain and fatigue rarely elevate a doctor to success. What are you doing each day for your health? Are you regenerating each day or degenerating?

Besides exercise and diet, what are you doing for your mental and physical health? When is your next vacation and where are you going? How many weeks of vacation are you doing this year? What about next year?

What techniques can you learn to enhance your practice and take stress off your joints as you age?

Are you connecting with those you love? Spending enough time with friends and family? What can you do to change this?

The greatest driver of your income, prosperity and long-term success is your health. If you tell your patients to exercise, do you exercise most days of the week?

When giving your patients nutritional advice, do you yourself follow your own recommendations? Are you aware of your own health markers? When did you last have comprehensive lab work done and what were your results? Is your good health a theory, or do you have numbers to prove it?

True story, my Mom experienced rheumatic fever as a child and was monitored by a cardiologist in her senior years. She outlived two different cardiologists that were each much younger than her...both dropped dead from heart attacks! Meanwhile, she lived to 91 following a chiropractic lifestyle!

In our town there is a 350+ pound obese practicing cardiologist. Do think his patients trust his recommendations? Probably not. Don't be that doc. Don't be a hypocrite, your patients can figure that out. Lead by example. Both of my Mom's former cardiologists left behind shocked families.

Besides your patients, who is depending on you? Did you know that chiropractors have alarmingly high disability rates? What would happen if you were disabled and could not work?

What can you change immediately to improve your health? What can you do in your practice to save your joints for decades? What can you do daily to promote long-term health for yourself?

Answer these questions honestly and act on them please doc, no matter what your age!

Chapter 32
OWN IT!

"Be sure the song you came to sing does not remain unsung."
– Ila Calton

Do you own it? You know what I am talking about...Do you OWN IT?

When you own it, you feel differently when you walk into your home, your shower, getting into your car, walking into your office, and walking into your adjusting room. Owning it totally changes your game. Owning it changes the outcome of the day, of the year and of your life. You can own it by making the decision to own it.

So, what does it mean to own it to you? Does it mean that you have all your ducks in a row for the day and your list is complete by sunset? Does it mean financially that you're set for the month and all bills are paid till next month or did you take the time and effort to make a future plan that is perfect for you?

Knowing your truth will completely set you up to own it. You can manifest your perfect world by knowing *your* truth, being grateful for it on the daily and knowing how it will feel to own it.

Practicing how it feels to own it will help you really own it in no time. What do you feel when you walk into a room and you have your truth inside your heart and mind and it's all set?

Empowering. Light. Strong. Sexy. Healthy. Rich.

When you take control and start creating your own narrative you will have your story unfold right before you. Then you will begin to Own It. Creating that story that is inside of you and only you.

Excellent marketing is great at this and it's so fun to watch. A story is created, and you actually want to become part of the story. You will dive right into the story and see yourself wearing that Rolex or driving that incredible sports car with the words that the marketer uses and the imagery that is in the ad. Incredible isn't it! You want to Own It just because that ad was awesome!

The feeling that is created can be re-created over and over. The universe is unlimited and generous when you ask. Your task is to know what to ask, then ask every day. To keep the blessings coming, you receive with gratitude and maintain that, and you will Own It. You'll own it ALL the time. Not just sometimes. ALL the Time!

Celebrate you and do this simple task daily and you will Own It. You'll have fun doing it, too. It's your story, so you create what story you want, give thanks as if it has already happened and you will Own It.

Guess what else will happen when you do this consistently? You become a magnet for new patients that love being around you. They will gladly pay you, refer to you and stay with you. Then more blessings come your way! Fun isn't it?

Chapter 33

MOOD RING MANAGEMENT

"When it's safe to talk about mistakes, people are more likely to report errors and less likely to make them."
– Sheryl Sandberg

Isn't it fun when the practice is humming? Lots of new patients, lots of patient visits, lots of great collections. Life is good, and the doctor is happy! And when the doctor is happy, the staff is happy. It really is like life in eutopia, or Camelot if you will.

Now what about when the practice is down? Stagnant numbers for new patients, falling patient visit numbers, low collections. Now what, Camelot is crushed? The doctor is likely unhappy, and the staff is stressed, possibly even feeling picked on. Conversely, the doctor feels like the staff is destroying their practice. Not a good scenario.

You see practices, like most things in life, follow trends. Practices go up and down. The trick is spotting a downward trend early and righting the ship before great damage is done. It is very tricky to have constant peak performance, in fact it is an art to accomplish. We are human and that means that it's tough to be on top of your game every single day. However, we can focus on being on point the majority of the time. Our success is dependent upon how effective we manage our practices daily.

So, what's the trick to managing a practice successfully?

Please understand this next statement doc because your success depends on it: Practices are either process driven or emotionally driven.

Most doctors manage by emotions which is hugely ineffective, and often destructive in the long-term. We call this "Mood Ring Management", something that your staff and patients cannot depend on. When the doc is in a good mood, everything hums. When the doc is in a bad mood, few good things happen.

Practices need to be process driven. Why? Because everyone knows what to expect, what to focus on and what to do when a downward trend is beginning.

What is a process driven practice? Simply put, it's a practice that is defined. All job duties and responsibilities are defined and laid out in a manual, otherwise known as standard operating procedures. The practice is driven and monitored by statistics so that trends can be spotted early and capitalized on or corrected. And all marketing is planned in advance, with clear objectives, and monitored for effectiveness.

Success is process driven, failure is emotionally driven. While it's true that we need good emotions in practice, the best way to get good emotions and keep them is to run a process driven practice.

Mood Ring Management benefits no one. Your staff and patients are left to wonder each day if it's a green ring day or a red ring day? Both your staff and patients need structure to flourish. While it takes time to plan and implement a process driven practice, the results are worth it!

So doc, slide that mood ring into a drawer and put it away for good. Initiate a process driven practice. Your staff, your patients, your bank account, and your sanity will thank you for it. The added bonus is that your career success depends on it.

Chapter 34

MARKETING TRUTH #7:

BE REMARKABLE

"Why fit in, when you were born to stand out?"
- Dr. Seuss

One of my favorite books of all time is Seth Godin's Purple Cow. Seth challenges us as business owners to infuse something "remarkable" into everything we do as a business. He is also a huge advocate for creating products and services that are worth marketing in the first place.

The subtitle of *Purple Cow* says it all: *Transform Your Business by Being Remarkable.* I can honestly say this principle, the chance to create something truly remarkable, is what motivates me to work every day and love what I do.

While old school marketing books teach us about the traditional 5 P's of marketing (every marketer has *favorite* five), which are based on a combination of factors, including product, pricing, positioning, promotion, publicity, packaging, pass-along, and permission, these are just that… old school.

More relevant and "now" are the concepts in marketing that matter. Why? Because there is a direct correlation to implementing these recommendations to follow and the results you will achieve both in your revenues and brand building.

- **Differentiate your customers.** Find the group that's most profitable. Find the group that's most likely to influence other customers. Figure out how to develop for, advertise to, or reward either group. Ignore the rest. Cater to the customers you would choose if you could choose your customers.
- Do you have the email addresses of the 20% of your customer base that loves what you do? If not, start getting them. If you do, what could you make for them that would be super special?
- Remarkable is about the small stuff. The way you answer the phone, launch a new service for your customers. Be fearless about testing out new things for your customers. Sometimes you'll win, sometimes you'll learn, but when it's for your customers, they will appreciate the effort.

- Find things that are "just not done" in your market, and then go ahead and do them.

For example, Southwest Airlines, when they first started made the idea of flying fun. I will never forget on a trip to Miami, at the beginning, through the flight and at the end, we were updated by a very colorful attendant who sang, did some beatboxing and hip hop opera to get people's attention. Boy was he remarkable. He got a hearty applause for his performance and warned us to stay in our seats instead of giving him the well-deserved standing ovation. Now that's remarkable!

Chapter 35

CREATING A TEAM SWEET SPOT

"Fight for the things that you care about, but do it in a way that will lead others to join you."
- Ruth Bader Ginsberg

Finding harmony in relationships is fun and also maddening! When the relationships are in an office setting, it can be extra hard because it can affect your bottom line.

There is a sweet spot in business relationships that can be found, and it takes time and effort from both parties. If you both come from a respectful position the relationship can begin to deepen and grow strong. Mutual trust and respect are the starter pack for relationship harmony.

Does your staff know the reason you became a Doctor of Chiropractic? The reason I am asking is because if your staff knows your "Why" they will understand why you do certain things in your office and it's much easier to have a harmonious relationship with them.

You also need to know their reasons for wanting to work for you. Is it the healing environment that enticed them to come on board to your office? Did they just want a 9-5 type job and that is why they are working for you? If you know the reasons why they want to work for you, then you both can be on the same page with each other about the direction of the office. It is important to be congruent about the reasons why that you both are in the office.

Another way to create harmony between you and your staff is to have each new staff member go through the new patient process within a few days of starting their job at your office. Your new hire begins the experience by calling your office like a regular new patient does.

They should receive a thorough history, exam and appropriate diagnostics, as indicated. Be respectful of employment laws, you cannot require a staff member to go under care, but you can have them experience a mock version of what a patient experiences for training purposes. This can be eye opening for you and the staff member. Many staff members are eager to learn about care and will gladly consent to care. The bonus is that through this exercise you will learn so much about them as a person and clinically it may explain some things you didn't know or understand regarding their health. The bottom line is that all of this gets you on the same page with your new staff member and brings them up to speed. If you do not train your new staff in this fashion, then they are left to guess at what you do. That should be enough motivation right there to complete this exercise!

Does your staff physically represent your office well? In other words, do they understand why chiropractic care is so crucial to health and wellness? You should be educating them every day on the benefits of the care you provide. In fact, the staff members often become such raving fans that I have heard of some of them actually go outside and call friends from their own cell phones to bring them into the office as new patients after getting their first adjustment.

A staff member's energy should be felt through the phone when they answer it at your office. You never want a low energy staff member taking phone calls. That first point of contact should be upbeat and welcoming and sound like a healthy person should sound! Prospective patients will have a mental idea of what your staff looks like when they talk to them over the phone and it should be a picture of a healthy person.

Helping staff prioritize their tasks is a great way to keep the lines of communication open and will result in a nice harmonic relationship between you and your team. How can you expect them to know what is important to you unless you tell them and help them make a list of priorities? Following up on these listed tasks is an obvious job for you and the follow up must be consistent. If you aren't consistent with following up on tasks with the staff, they will wrongly assume that the task wasn't as important to you as it once was. If you communicate this thoroughly and the team understands what you'd like to have happen every week, the office will be a well highly efficient and fun place to go to every day for all involved.

Last but not least, let's talk about how your staff handle your money and how a great, clear understanding from both sides is absolutely necessary. Eventually your staff will come in contact with your money. Because you will train them correctly, they will look at this part of their job as a major component of the business and understand your expectations regarding money. I explain it to my staff very simply when I train them about money. I let them know that I will pay them every single payroll with passion, commitment and great energy. I let them know that I expect to be paid the same way. When they are in charge of collecting from a patient, any amount whatsoever, I expect the same passion, commitment and energy in return. You don't drop the ball and skip a paycheck to your staff, so they can't drop the ball and skip collecting from a patient under any circumstance. It isn't their decision to make to let a patient skip a payment. If there is an issue with a patient making a payment, then a different payment schedule must be cleared through you. Only you can decide if a payment is altered in any way, not your staff. The doctor creates the payment details, no one else, and that is non-negotiable.

So, let's face it, the inner workings of staff relationships are so mega important to the success of your office. Richard Branson says you must come from a point of mutual compassionate directness. What a great way to describe how to be gently direct with respect and still get things at the office done effectively and efficiently. Compassionate directness can put a great relationship in a sweet spot so that the work, chiropractic, can be the priority for the patient. At the end of the day that is what the patient needs; a team that stays congruent with all ideals of the office which is to provide an awesome, healthy experience with the patient's needs at the top of the list.

Chapter 36
LIKE STEVE MCQUEEN...

*"Your faith can move mountains
and your doubt can create them."*
- Unknown

Ever listen to "Steve McQueen", the song sung by Sheryl Crow?

That's a great effing song! Sheryl Crow nailed that song, and everyone can feel like a rock star while they are drumming on the steering wheel listening to that song cranked up to 11! No one was cooler than Steve McQueen!

Hey! Maybe we should listen to that song more carefully.

Sheryl Crowe was thinking *like* Steve McQueen. She's not Steve McQueen obviously but she's *thinking* like him and that song went up the charts like a rocket.

I'm saying she's onto something. Thinking *like* we are something is powerful. Thinking is where it's at! Haven't you heard the saying "if you think you can, you can"? I'm into it!

You could think you have the best, most successful, profitable practice and eventually it'll happen.

That's the way your heroes think, I promise.

You can't beat the law of attraction. Use it to your advantage. It's science and it works every single time. What is in your subconscious mind will rock you to the next level or destroy you.

Shift your thinking to one of success and prosperity only. Nothing else. What will happen next will be predictable, exciting, sexy, addicting and something you will want to repeat over and over. The way you think is a decision, an exact behavior. You can keep it on repeat and have success over and over.

What would your life be like if you really didn't get attached to the outcome of the day?

If you were given a hypothetical blank check and you were told that it couldn't be written for too much, you just had to think positively: What would your life really turn out like?

Oftentimes, the way you process things and the way you think is a habit. It's likely related to how you were brought up and, that is how you've "always" thought. The sad fact is that some of you are certain you can never change. Those of you that are successful **know** that you can adapt and meld into whatever mindset you need to for success.

There was a young person in a big city during the depression that dreamed of starting a business and becoming rich beyond measure. All he thought he needed was capital.

A very successful, experienced local businessman heard about the young budding entrepreneur and went to find out all about it.

When they met the dreamer asked for advice about how he could get his dream in motion. The experienced man thought about it and told him that he would be glad to help him out. He handed the young man a blank check and told him that if he absolutely had to, he could fill out the check himself and he could cash it. He told the dreamer that he couldn't write the check for too much. He could only use it if he had NO other options and he had exhausted every other opportunity for success. The dreamer was happy to agree to the small condition and put the check in his wallet.

The story goes that years and years later a very successful millionaire passed away and a family member found a blank check from years and years before written by John D. Rockefeller in the deceased millionaire's wallet. The young dreamer met a very successful person (Rockefeller) and did exactly what he was told to do. He never had to cash that unlimited check because **HE** was his own *source* for success!

Proof that the young budding entrepreneur thought his way to success and the lack of capital was not his problem at all.

You too can think like a successful dreamer! Then you will become the real success that you've envisioned for yourself!

Chapter 37

PULL THAT RIPCORD!

"Until you are ready to look foolish, you'll never have the possibility of being great."

- Cher

What are you waiting for?

Go ahead...PULL that RIPCORD!!

What's the number one reason doctors aren't successful in practice? We can all start listing reasons. Maybe they don't have enough capital. Maybe it's a bad location. Maybe they need that one more piece of equipment that would really put them over the top.

So, what we are talking about is resources. Are we saying that if the doctor had more resources they'd be successful?

I call BS!!

YOU are the source of all resources. It's you and a healthy dose of confidence that the practice needs. Nothing more. That is the magic of our craft.

Our success is wrapped around our ability to hold our mind around the fact that we CAN and SHOULD have success. We deserve it.

Self Esteem. That's not so hard to wrap our mind around then is it?

Our self-esteem will either have our foot on the gas or the brake. Not both. Where is your foot?

If you think that your practice should do without advertising while you are growing your practice, you are doing without. You don't have to do without while you're gaining success.

If you think you shouldn't buy a piece of equipment while you're gaining success because you're not sure if you can make the payment, let the patients make the payments and get the piece of equipment. My mentor taught me that I should "make so much money, it doesn't matter!" Good Answer!

Have the mindset that you already are successful. Then you will be. You can think yourself to success. Many do. It's a decision.

It is about a healthy amount of self-esteem.

PULL that RIPCORD!!

Chapter 38

MARKETING TRUTH #8:

HOW TO CREATE AN OFFER, THE RIGHT WAY!

*"It's not about selling,
it's about creating value for your audience"*
- J.Allocca

Working with one of my clients, she was starting to explore the idea of marketing for her business. She had been promoting her business with flyers, in the local small newspaper and the like. She didn't really have a marketing strategy and didn't understand the return on investment for her marketing efforts. Sound familiar?

Random acts of marketing unfortunately don't work because there is no way to track trends, what worked, what didn't, why it worked, etc., Same goes for putting together a proper offer. You have to test and tweak, which is often my answer. What I can say is that you want to stay clear of selling products and services. What???

Yes, I said it, STOP SELLING Products and Services! No, I'm not sniffing glue and my ginkgo supplement is working just fine. What I mean is that you want to reframe selling by selling offers. An offer is something chock full of value that becomes a no-brainer when you present the price. Why? Because the value far and away exceeds the price. When the value is clearly articulated and understood by the right customers, the price doesn't matter.

Let's go back to my client. She had recently completed a training that was already being implemented in her practice. She was not charging for it, instead was just giving more value. The problem is that the value was not understood by the customer.

So, I challenged her to create an offer for her email list of customers. The way to make it enticing was to create a bundled offer. What else could she bundle together along with this new technique she had learned? So, we explored complementary add-ons. We bundled together three offerings into one bundle, priced it at a very healthy margin and promoted to her list.

Now it wasn't about "how much is it?" and selling the one service. It was about selling the transformation of why her customer would benefit by the three modalities in one. The focus was on the aggregate value of having these three techniques work synergistically and why the customer would benefit from this specific offer. It was a very powerful reframe. Long story short, she sold her new bundle offer and was pleasantly surprised with the outcome. The marketing light went on and the rest is history.

Sell offers! Not products and services.

Chapter 39
CREATING FREEDOM

*"Normal is not something to aspire to,
it's something to get away from."
– Jodi Foster*

When you look at a bird's eye view of your practice, what do you see? A well-oiled healing, profitable, sustainable machine with systems, clinical and business protocols in place?

If that is true, this chapter is not for you...honestly, it just isn't.

However, if you are the doctor that has your mind open and you are willing to look at things from all sides, keep reading!

The case types you accept in your office should be based on several things. Like, what type of patient do you like to see, what case types are the most fun, and what case types are the most profitable? All those questions are great questions to define and you should have a system and protocol in place for each case type. Notice that we didn't ask what types of case that you are afraid of.

For example, a PI patient's case may be more complicated paper work wise, clinically it could more complicated as well, and the paper trail may be quite a bit different. When you look at the profitability of a PI case, it should be your highest comparatively due to the complexity. Often these cases require more hours, more high-level clinical decisions, and you should get paid accordingly. It's imperative that you are able to diagnose and treat these patients correctly. PI cases can be lucrative, loads of fun and, to the patient, it can mean the world that you accepted the case and helped them like no one else could. All in all, PI cases can be very rewarding.

So many doctors are intimidated by a PI case and afraid to help these patients. Many think that they will have mountains of paperwork, a whiney patient, and will end up having to reduce their fees. If you do PI correctly, none of that is the usual and customary outcome. Your state has specific laws regarding accident claims, and it is good to know what they are. If the laws aren't PI friendly, the laws may in fact change. If they are friendly to PI cases, then why turn away money when it walks in the door? Learn how to handle a PI case from the first day they walk into the office to closing the case. Understand how to perform diagnostic testing that shows the trauma and allows you to diagnose and treat all the injuries correctly. You should be able to explain these studies so that a 6th grader can understand them. Most of these patients have very few people in their corner. You can be a huge help to these folks.

Attorneys love working with first class, smart doctors but will not work with an inefficient, poorly managed chiropractic office. Many attorneys have very few top-notch chiropractors to work with, so the competition is limited. You can certainly carve out a part of the market by being the awesome chiropractor that you are and adding another income stream at the same time. That is a great thing for your office and your community. There are many excellent resources for learning how to diagnose, treat and manage PI cases correctly. The only limitation to being excellent at PI is you!

Do you enjoy cash patients? Why wouldn't you enjoy a patient that pays cash whether it's at the time of service or if they pay in advance? There is a different level of commitment from a patient that is a cash payer. They tend to be great referral sources, too. While we are talking about referrals, that reminds us of the Medicare patient. They are the best referral sources in our office and probably in yours, too. That is, if you aren't afraid to take Medicare cases. If you aren't accepting Medicare patients, you might consider taking those cases as a non-participant. Keep it simple for you and your staff. These folks get the worst care for their spines outside of chiropractic and so many can certainly benefit from being consistent chiropractic patients.

Business wise it is a great idea to balance your office with multiple case types. There are advantages of having each type of case. If a certain type of case brings in money and helps the patient, why would you turn it away and not accept it? It happens all the time in our profession. We talk our way out of helping people and making money. You can think of a ton of reasons why you shouldn't accept certain types of cases. The truth is that when you turn away a case without a valid reason, you are turning away money.

You should never say no to money. When you close the door to one "type" of money, you are closing the door to all types of money. Keeping the flow of money open and coming toward you like the strongest magnet will launch your practice into orbit. When the numbers of a practice increase, the morale of the doctor improves, as well as the staff's morale. When the morale of everyone is great, the stress can be reduced, and the energy goes up. The focus of the doctor can instantly improve and life in the office can be fun again! This can affect profitability and eventually sustainability of your practice. As all of this becomes a habit, then you'll see the office repeating the cycle. A truly successful office can be on a semi autopilot mode because of the systems in place and the consistency of implementing these systems will make the outcomes consistent.

The awesome cycle of predictability and routine will help your office be the ultimate place of healing that you've dreamed of your entire career and you will be closer and closer to the Freedom in and out of practice you didn't know you could achieve.

Chapter 40

IF ALL YOU HAVE IS A HAMMER, THEN EVERYTHING IS A NAIL

"I'm always inspired by actresses who are older than me. Because I know that person has lived so much more life than I have. There's a whole other toolbox."
– Kate Winslet

When you get past 15 years or so of practice, it is amazing how many of your classmates are no longer practicing. Some develop physical disabilities. Many simply burn out.

A key to staying excited and engaged in the game is to continually develop new skills. The icing on the cake is that when you develop new skills, you often add increased revenue to your practice. Simply by your mental engagement and enthusiasm. Your patients feel it and engage with it, and your practice soars!

Additionally, you may learn new techniques or strategies that allow you to practice effectively and protect your body as you age.

Your best investment long-term is in yourself. Keep investing in yourself. Keep learning. The more tools you have in your toolbox, the greater ability you have to serve your patients. And you avoid burn out.

If all you have is a hammer to work with, then everything you run across is a nail. Who wants to look at nails all day long, every single day? Expand your mind, expand your skills and you expand your practice.

What can you learn today to feed your brain and your practice? What areas of excellence do you wish to develop in your skill set? Who benefits from your increased knowledge base? What new revenue streams will be created by what you learn?

Targeted learning ignites you and your practice!

Chapter 41
HEADSPACE 101

"Every day, stand guard at the door of your mind."
-Jim Rohn

What you think about you bring about…no truer words have ever been spoken. Our thoughts seed the path forward. Often doctors fail in practice long before they ever get the wheels up in a practice because they've defeated themselves with poor thinking. Negative thoughts clog your brain and don't allow you to see the opportunities ahead and solutions to the challenges at hand.

Your subconscious mind is a powerful force that can lead you to unlimited success or predictable failure. Have you ever watched an elite athlete prepare to compete? Pay attention to greatness. At that level of competition, often the winning difference is headspace. The athlete will mentally walk themselves through every step to victory prior to competing. They literally see the victory ahead of time.

How many times do you see victory when you sit in your initial consultation with a new patient? Do you mentally expect success? Or, are you filled with unspoken questions about your communication strategies and abilities to serve your new patient? What is the dialogue running through your mind?

When you have self-defeating chatter going on in your head it does not allow you to connect and get on the same page with your patient. Often doctors are so used to their self-defeating thoughts that they don't outwardly hear them.

Eleanor Roosevelt said it best: "I'm just going to try to stay out of my own way."

When our greatest obstacle is our self, the patient never has a chance to get in the way. We will beat them to the punch.

There are two realities in every situation: the one that stops us, and the solution that propels us. Your subconscious mind decides which path you take. You either see possibilities or roadblocks. One energizes you, the other drains you.

How well do you take care of your subconscious mind? What do you let in?

What do you feed it? And how do you protect it?

Answer carefully for therein lies an enormous key to your lifelong success.

Chapter 42
MARKETING TRUTH #9: JUST ASK.

"Here's the big secret… people don't know what they want"
- R. Levesque

JUST ASK.

When was the last time you asked your customers what they want? Most business owners skip the fountain of gold they are sitting on. Asking their customers for what would help them. Just Ask. The ASK Method is a popular marketing strategy created by Ryan Levesque. The premise is simple, ask your customers what they want and then create it and sell to them.

Here are some steps to take to create a survey for your customers to find out what they want:

Step 1: The first step is all about knowing your audience and understanding what they really want by sending a survey to your current customer list. Ask them: "What is your biggest challenge with (insert your service)?"

When you receive the results, something miraculous happens. You get to know first-hand the pain points of your target marketing and it is all written in their language, or how they would refer to the problem. This helps you map out what comes next...

Step 2: Segment the topics that you observe over and over again by reviewing the survey responses. In reviewing the feedback, you will see specific language trends, topic trends, interest trends. Create buckets from those themes. For example, if you are a chiropractor and you found that people typically call your business for back pain | nutrition counseling | sports injuries, you would segment your business into those three sections.

Each of these sections can be clickable online, leading to a different landing page and experience for each type of customer.

Step 3: You can take segmentation a step further, by tailoring your offering to the specific type of customer. Let's say a prospective customer visits your website, they will be "prescribed," or they will receive a different set of emails depending on their interest. The information is highly relevant to their needs, interests and pain points.

Remember to "test & tweak" along the way. Pivot when necessary, always referring back to your customer's needs. Ask yourself, "is this going to serve my customers?"

Chapter 43

BE AFRAID, VERY AFRAID OF THE SCARCITY MINDSET

"If you keep saying things are going to be bad, you have a good chance of being a prophet."
– Isaac Bashevis Singer

Scarcity is a terrible place to hang out in!

If it's so terrible then why do we go there?

Haven't you heard lots of chiropractors hanging out and talking about how bad things are? How the medical profession is trying to get rid of chiropractic, how there are not enough new patients, and how they are "just" chiropractors!

WTH?

They are so serious it is scary. It is scary because it isn't true! AT ALL!

I was taught that "you bring about what you think about". It is obvious what they are thinking about all the time.

There is a chiropractor that I know that was basically homeless and he worked his tail off with smart efforts and a "won't quit" attitude and is one of the most successful DC's that I know. In his mind he never allowed a negative thought, a scarcity thought to camp out and stay. He only saw success and prosperity. He knew in his heart that he had the secret to health right in his hands and had the passion and "stick to it" energy to share it with everyone he met. There were plenty of reasons for him to give up, lose focus and actually quit being a chiropractor. Yet, he never ever gave up.

It's easy to point the finger at someone else though, isn't it?

What is your mindset like on a daily basis? What do you allow your brain to focus on every day, every week, every month, every year?

When you look back at your practice last year, what do you see? Is it a productive, rocking place of health? Is it as full and prosperous as you want it to be? Are you of service to many? Are you living the dream life and loving what you are put on this earth to do?

When you can say, "Yes!" to all of those questions, then it absolutely sounds like you have a zero scarcity mindset. Congratulations!

Now on to the rest of the group!

If you are not where you want to be, or your office isn't hitting the goals you want it to knock down, or if your life isn't fulfilled by dressing up, showing up and being a smart enthusiastic chiropractor, let's get some real talk going then!

Here's the thing...you must not ever allow scarcity to park in your mind rent free. That is a NO GO! We all have doubts and crummy moments and maybe even an off day, but you can't allow scarcity to take root in your mind. One doubt can allow more doubts, that can quickly lead to a "lack" mentality. NOTHING grows in that garden! You have the potential to have all, and be all, to the sick and challenged people on this earth. You MUST be a serious warrior against scarcity. If you aren't in warrior mode, and you lose focus, it's easy for the mind to wander down that dark path of scarcity.

You've seen it many times over in our profession. You've seen a really bright doctor with amazing talents and they can barely make rent. You see them eventually leave our blessed profession...another sad statistic.

It's a head game and if you deny that truth, you could be a statistic too.

So, what is the secret to avoid scarcity? It's more than just one thing. Our minds are such complicated computers on one hand and then on another, it's simple.

A daily list of what we are wanting to achieve, read daily, is the best start! Keep it in your pocket, billfold, somewhere that's handy so that you can read it three times a day and only focus on those goals getting accomplished. See what it looks like in your mind's eye when you've gotten the goal accomplished. Never get caught up in how they will get accomplished but only **why** they will get accomplished.

The "why" is what gives the goal the *muscle* and *energy* to soar! You have this potential inside already sitting there waiting to be called upon. Your subconscious mind will either think there is a zero there or there is a great list of goals to achieve. It can't think of anything in between. Your subconscious has no sense of humor either. When you say things in jest that are self-deprecating, you cement that into your subconscious mind and it is there to wreak havoc on all the good things that you have already put into your head. My mentor would always tell me that negative thoughts can't live in your head "rent free"! What he meant was to give those thoughts the boot as soon as you realize that they are setting up house!

There are plenty of consequences to a scarcity mindset in chiropractic as a whole.

The absolute worst consequence is the death of a beautiful, lifesaving profession called Chiropractic.

That is a sad thought, isn't it?

That is not something you should have to think about. Nor should you even have to battle it, but the truth is that it's out in this world by the ton and you must be ready to battle it like a champ.

You must have No Mercy, No Quarter.

Now be your best, most brilliant self and take action against scarcity.

Chapter 44

DO YOU HAVE A STAFF INFECTION?

"Daring leaders are never silent about hard things."
– Brene Brown

We all do at some point in our practices!! It's a matter of how fast we get through it and with as little collateral damage as possible.

Recently, I experienced a painful staff infection and I'd like to share it with you.

My front desk CA, (we will call her Angela out of respect for her) was talking to a patient about scheduling and about our calendar. Angela told the patient that I would be "out of town" on this certain day and "we would NOT be open", that we would be "CLOSED" and the "next available appointments would be Monday". Mind you, the patient never ASKED for this information, instead Angela volunteered the information and made it the focus of the conversation.

I exploded!! Why do you ask? Because she was totally focused on the negative, operating out of fear and had a "lack" mentality. The mindset she was operating under will destroy a practice!! Remember to train your staff to tell the patient what you CAN do for them, not what you CAN'T do. Positive headspace is where it's at!!

So, when certain people get an infection, they go get antibiotics and go the medical route. When chiropractors get an infection, we get adjusted...over and over again until we beat it. We are super smart about this!

It was obvious to me that Angela needed a headspace adjustment and needed more than just one, as soon as possible, or my practice would certainly suffer permanent damage.

We sat down and I began to ask her questions. I know her history and her background and it made sense why she operated out a "lack of" system, and it was time to begin the headspace adjustments. She has struggled with many challenges and also is an awesome friend to many, beautiful inside and out. She has been involved in chiropractic for years.

I asked her to tell me what she thought about her comments to the patient and she completely understood that she was being very negative and that she was in a fearful mode. Fearful that the patient wouldn't reschedule and keep their care plan, that the stats would look terrible and I would go crazy over a lost patient and a refund would make it sting even more. It went exactly how she expected it to go…BADLY!! She got exactly what she expected.

She is a visual learner so here came the lesson…

I wrote down four simple math problems on a piece of paper and I intentionally wrote the first one wrong and the next three right. I asked her to tell me what she saw. She instantly told me that the first problem was wrong. That is all she said, even after some prodding, she told me again the "first problem is wrong".

Wow!! So here is the first headspace adjustment for Angela!!

I asked her why she only focused on the wrong one and she emphatically told me that the others were right, BUT the first one was "WRONG"!

I asked her what would happen if she did four things for me and three were right, but only one was wrong and I focused on the wrong one and never mentioned the three things that she did that were right? "Angela, what if I managed you that way?" I asked her how that would feel?

The light came on and I just adjusted her above the atlas, so to speak.

To get some further healing done, I asked her if she wanted patients to really look at us as if we were ONLY open on this certain day or CLOSED on a certain day, or did she really want patients to see us in their minds as OPEN and ready to serve them?

She felt another adjustment! And we were gaining on it, folks!

I explained to her some of her life problems were because 75% of the time she operated in a mentality that drove negativity and a poverty lifestyle right back to her. This is tough for anyone to admit and she is a great person and really is bright. She knew this but didn't have a handle on how to correct it.

I asked her what she had to lose if she let go of the old way of thinking and looked at everything from a prosperity model.

Another adjustment delivered!! She was growing, I could see it! She knew she only had wonderful things to gain and only garbage to lose.

We see our staff do this type of thinking all the time, but let's be honest with ourselves: How many of you docs out there come from a headspace of lack, poverty, negativity, and/or a downright awful place?

We all are human and have been there. The winners will only sit there momentarily, and self-correct very, very quickly. It's human nature to occasionally have a Pity Party, but we can't hang out there all day!! Feel it and move on!! Get outta there as soon as you feel it coming on.

As we grow in life and in practice, we learn when we need our headspace adjusted. We also learn about our staff infections and that our staff need to be adjusted just like we do. We all need occasional course corrections.

Do that headspace adjustment frequently docs, and don't let this happen to you. There is abundance and prosperity for everyone, go out there and make it happen!!

Chapter 45
THE LONG VIEW

"My life is my message."
- Mahatma Gandhi

Successful people plan for generations. They create dynasties. The unsuccessful plan for Saturday night. You must develop the long view. Conceptualize your ability to succeed and the steps to get there.

Make clear, objective, measurable goals with time frames. Think about your future. See it. Feel it. Hear it. Smell it. Taste it. Ask yourself: what will have to happen in order for me to get there? Not pie in the sky, ask yourself definitive questions.

Plan, plan, plan. Accept mis-takes and make course corrections. None of us are infallible, we all make mistakes, but they are actually mis-takes. Learn from your mis-takes instead of beating yourself up over them. Take what you have learned and make the necessary course corrections to get back on track and not repeat the same lesson. Mis-takes make us wiser, make us stronger and actually move us closer to success. Embrace not being perfect and celebrate mis-takes by using them to propel you forward!

Few people get rich quick, so plan for the long haul. There is excitement in moving towards the life of your dreams. Enjoy every moment because you've earned it. Luck is of course wonderful; most people get luckier the more committed that they are to their work! Samuel Goldwyn said it best: "The harder I work, the luckier I get."

Many successful people have mentors and coaches to help keep them on task and on track to achieve their goals. Who do you trust to mentor you? If you don't have a mentor, who will call you out on your B.S.? Who will show you shortcuts or do you want to re-invent wheels? Which innovator will show you solutions that you do not yet know are possible?

Get out of the day to day struggles. Develop your long view, create your vision and move toward it! The end result is that the day to day struggles dissolve in the light of your committed vision!

Chapter 46
DON'T HIRE CHELSEA

"Great vision without great people is irrelevant."
- Jim Collins

Recently we had a great laugh with a doctor and staff that we are mentoring. We were discussing hiring and someone in the room blurted out: "Don't hire Chelsea. Every Chelsea we've ever hired has not worked out."

So, who is Chelsea?

Perhaps the staff member that ran all the new patients off because she talked them out of chiropractic care.

Or maybe the front desk person that was so extroverted that everything was about her and the practice dropped because the patients had enough of her and just couldn't stomach another story by Chelsea about Chelsea...

Then again, Chelsea could be the self-important, least experienced team member that feels that you are blessed to have her in the building, yet has no work ethic, and no integrity to call when she no-shows or is late for work.

If only it were that simple...just don't hire Chelsea. Problem solved. Yet, it's not that simple.

Hiring a team is one of the ways that you can leverage your time and scale your business. One of the important lessons we've learned is to hire slow and fire fast. Sounds harsh, but it is possible with a series of careful pre-screenings to recognize those people that are going to be a complement to your team.

The first is to share with a prospective hire your core values. The core values as cheesy and outdated as it may sound should be considered the guiding principles for your business's reason for being.

Now this is not one of those sterile corporate mission statements which includes words such as "infrastructure, optimization, synergistically" and other twenty-five cent words that are intended to make them sound smart but lack true human connection.

Think about the core values of your business, what are the values that come to mind for why you are in business. The Indie Docs core values are clear: health, peace and freedom. They show up in everything we do, why we do it and for what purpose.

So, once you have your core values, we encourage you to tap into the various assessments available online including Myers-Briggs, Enneagram, Wealth Test to name a few. The goal is to assess the personality type that would be the perfect fit for the role you have available. By the way docs, please map out and define the traits that you are looking for in each staff position in your office. Are you looking for an outgoing, persuasive extrovert? Do you need a left-brained analytical, attention to detail ninja? By having these assessments as one point of the screening process, you will start to understand how that candidate is wired, how they like to receive information and how they would potentially fit into your organization.

By doing this exercise, you will not only be able to assess who would be a good fit for your culture, you'll also know how to best communicate with them.

Chapter 47

THE WORD "CLOSE" IN CHIROPRACTIC

*"If we want to have the biggest impact,
the best way to do this is to make sure we always focus on
solving the most important problems."*
– Mark Zuckerberg

That is a hot topic isn't it?

Terms and phrases like "closer", "closing for Chiropractic", and "closed for care" are sure being thrown around a lot. Been there, done that.

The term is not for everyone, many doctors say it really grates on their nerves. So much in fact, that some doctors are using the phrase "opening for chiropractic" to mean virtually the same thing.

Having used the terminology before and moving past the concept ourselves, we have a few theories about why many doctors don't like the term "close". Some may be sensitive to our words here, please hear us out.

"Close" has a salesman feel, it also has a negative connotation of being snagged or captured. Is this your favorite comparison? It isn't our favorite comparison either.

Could it be because the persona of a salesperson is that they are not typically genuine, are trying to get me interested in something I don't really need, seem kinda slimy and usually are out primarily for the profit? Probably so. Obviously, when you are a "closer", regardless of your activity, you can certainly be thrown in a salesperson category.

Great products need promotion. Greatness alone does not assure success in any marketplace. Think about high-end goods like Rolex, Canada Goose and Mercedes Benz. Do you mind these three companies "selling" you their goods? NO. You don't mind it at all because you know there is mega-quality in all three of those products. All three products are a tremendous commercial success and guess what? They are Proud of it! However, they do not refer to themselves as "closers".

They are masters at producing a high-quality product. Equally as important, they are masters at communicating the value and significance of their high-quality contribution to your life. They set themselves apart. In reality, it's push versus pull marketing. You desire and seek them out, versus a salesperson convincing you that you need them.

How do you feel when you wear a Rolex, with a Canada Goose jacket on while driving your Benz? You probably feel like a BOSS, totally cool and very successful. There are some very special things that each of these companies do to make sure they are viewed as top of the line, and an upper echelon experience.

Do you do these same things in your practice? Are you smart like Rolex? Are you communicating value, ethics, the highest standards of care? Are you the solution that your patient cannot find anywhere else?

If you are a great chiropractor, you should be a great communicator, right?

Your patients feel the same about you as they do for Rolex, Canada Goose or Mercedes Benz. They LOVE you! That is why they return and refer to you for years!

You can be a great doctor from a technical skills standpoint, but to be successful, you'd better be a master at communicating the significance and value of your care. It would be wise to focus on your communication skills. It would also be wise to understand what sets you apart in the marketplace.

Why are Rolex, Canada Goose and Mercedes Benz at the top of their games? Because they have redefined excellence and found a way to make us understand their value through communicating what sets them apart from their competition.

There is nothing wrong with being paid a premium for your product: quality, solution-oriented patient care, just as Rolex, Canada Goose and Mercedes Benz are paid for their excellent quality products.

Your patients are grateful that you are bold, confident, successful and a Rockstar smart doctor that delivered the solution to their problem and is worth every dang penny for care!

If you keep your ethics in check, your integrity above board and your patient's best interest first, you will deliver that value-added, high quality service everyone is seeking in every aspect of their life.

We should be thinking about our patients and the value of chiropractic on a larger scale versus patting ourselves on the back in any way. It's not about you, it's about the solution that you can provide to your patient. If you know that you can help your patient, then you have a moral obligation to deliver it to them because the solution to their problem is your services...chiropractic.

The question is then, how do we ethically provide our services in a real-world marketplace? At the end of the day, we must be a for profit business to be able to provide our services tomorrow. Chiropractic has both opportunities and challenges. Perception is powerful, and perception often becomes reality. How many times have we inadvertently created a perception different than we desire or hope without even realizing it?

The best way to provide your services is to be a great doctor and a great communicator, and to understand the unique value of your care. I would much rather be referred to as a "healer" than a "salesperson". I would much rather be the doctor that people seek out for care, rather than the doctor that needs to convince people about the value of any care or service. Again, it's a pull versus push mentality.

It's time to get back to being a great Doctor. Why do people become fans of the doctor shows on TV? Because we want someone to care about us. We want a Doctor that we can trust and one that communicates with us. Your patients are no different.

Being paid well for a quality service and being the solution for our patients should be a given. Being a great communicator so that our patients understand the value and significance of chiropractic care for their health and the relation to every facet of their life and future life with chiropractic should be a given. Therefore, patients committing themselves to their health physically, emotionally and financially should also be a given.

Instead of focusing on "salesperson logic", how about focusing on the global impact of chiropractic on humanity…starting with becoming the irreplaceable solution for the patient that sits in front of you?

Chapter 48

AWAKEN THE SLEEPING GIANT

*"Believe in something larger than yourself
…get involved in the big ideas of your time."
– Barbara Bush*

Recently, USA Today news posted a great article about life expectancy dropping in the United States. This crisis is due in a large part to the opioid epidemic.

The article was full of juicy pull quotes:

"Health researchers have some grim news for Americans: We are dying younger, and life expectancy is now down for the second straight year — something not seen in more than half a century."

"The declines are shockingly out of sync with a larger world in which lives are getting longer and healthier, public health experts said."

"The rest of the world is improving. The rest of the world is seeing large declines in mortality and large improvements in life expectancy," said Peter Muennig, a professor of health policy and management at Columbia University. "That's true in rich countries and middle-income countries and generally true even in lower-income countries."

"The difference between the U.S. and most of the rest of the world "is very stark," said Jonathan Skinner, a professor of economics at Dartmouth College."

Are you asking the larger question? Why are Americans taking opioids in the first place?

While it's true that chiropractic is not about pain, marketing is about positioning and perspective. The door is open to start asking why Americans are in so much pain that they're literally killing themselves with opioids? And by the way, their pain is physical and psychological.

The public may still have chiropractic skeptics, so let's help them. Skeptics may question chiropractic, but they also value data. Particularly when that data comes from respected medical resources like Columbia and Dartmouth researchers.

Your patients and the public have a sleeping giant within them. They are ready to jump on a cause and rally for you. They are tired of people dying. Nearly every one of them knows someone lost to opioids. The time is now. Are you ready to awaken the sleeping giant within them? It's time to bring awareness to them and allow them to take action. Make them aware not only of the problem, but also of the alternatives and solutions. Chiropractic, BOOM!

There are incredible internal and external marketing opportunities sitting there like low hanging fruit.

And the gift of this is TIMING...an astute marketers DREAM.

The media has brought us the whole thing on a silver platter! It's end of year. It's the holidays! People are coming together with those that they love and care about. What a great time to pass on valuable information! If nothing else, find a great informative article, print and hand it out. Highlight the pull quotes. Start the conversation and awareness. For example: "Mary so many families have been affected by this, will you help me get the word out?"

And those pesky New Year's Resolutions are right around the corner for our patients. Have you started a New Year, New You campaign? Are you doing not only classes on new patient orientation that get the word out, and also classes such as:

Stop Your Pain Now

Eat This, Not That

Alzheimer's and Dementia Prevention

Reducing Your Cancer Risk

The Cholesterol Myth

Boost Your Immunity

Improving Your Sleep

Why Are You So Tired? Get Your Energy Back

The possibilities are endless.....

Limits in this beautiful opportunity are YOU. Are you ready to step up to the plate and be the DOCTOR that your patients won't live without? You have a sleeping giant within you. It's time to awaken that giant. It's time to meet your destiny and live your dreams. This is your year to break the chains that bind you. Speak up and act out what's in you. Playing small doesn't save lives.

I can assure you of one thing for certain...THERE HAS NEVER BEEN A BETTER TIME TO BE A CHIROPRACTOR!

So PLEASE, Awaken the Giants within yourself, your patients and the public for the good of humankind.

Chapter 49

RELENTLESS

"This is who the fuck I am."
– *Lady Gaga*

We balance life between many responsibilities like: work, kids, money, spouse/love interest and friends. We can be too generous in our personal life and let the spouse/love interest take advantage of us and at the office we are rock stars with high volume and high collections.

How does this happen?

Or...we are only doing so-so at the office, living check to check is the norm and see average or low volumes with inconsistent new patient numbers with huge amounts of stress.

How, again, does this happen?

We can lose our balance so easily sometimes. It doesn't matter how smart we are, how good of a chiropractor that we are, how good of a money manager that we are, this can happen. Depending on your age and experience, many of us have been there and done it. Apologizing for making great money, healing people all day, keeping kids fed and watered isn't what should be happening.

Success is a circle. We know success and we breathe success every day in many ways. For some reason in certain categories we don't have the same success as we do in other categories.

For example, I know an awesome chiropractor that is a beautiful single mom, has a rocking high volume, high collection single doctor office. In her personal life, she is a tangled mess. She dates losers that are mostly unemployed, hustlers that leave her with a broken heart. She has it going her way in so many categories but not in the "love" category.

Then another example is that there's another DC that I know that has a very average office collections wise, pretty low volume, complains about staff, is always stressed about having no money and has the greatest marriage you can ever dream of.

Wow! Two different stories and the truth is that the solution is the same for both issues. Both women are really successful in two different categories but not in all the categories that they want success in.

What it comes down to is being **relentless**. We would never put up with xxx at the office if we are super rocks stars at the office, but we put up with lots of xxx at home. Our standards are not the same for some reason. That can change. Being as relentless at home with our heart for example is how we become successful in that arena.

Success has the same characteristics at home as it does at the office and vice versa. Why would we run a tight ship at home, but loosey-goosey at the office. We need to use those same organized, relentless home boss skills at the office as we do at home.

Have you ever heard of the saying, "Run it like a business"? I have also heard that if you don't do that, the same business could be only a hobby. What the saying is trying to convey, in my mind, is that we must run our business organized, squared away, systematically & logically.

Sun Tzu, The Art of War author states, "Let your plans be dark and impenetrable as night, and when you move, fall like a thunderbolt." That strategy is awesome for business, but we would never take that model into our personal relationships, or should we?

If we were as relentless in our personal lives as we are in running our business would we still be successful?

I think we could, if we are ruling with gentle hand and keeping in mind that we have priorities.

Our priority in our personal lives should be keeping our heart open yet protected. We have to make tough decisions about who has our best interests at heart. If we can logically see that our love interest doesn't have the same priorities, we must evaluate that as quickly as we would our lack of new patients in our business for example.

We can have success in all parts of our lives, but we must open the door for the person that we are equal to, not the person that brings us down. Our partner in life will lock arms with us and cheer us to the finish line personally and professionally. We should accept nothing less. We won't apologize for demanding it all. We are deserving of such and will not settle.

Be relentless.

Chapter 50

GOIN' NOWHERE?

"The world is the great gymnasium where we come to make ourselves strong."
– Swami Vivekananda

I was driving into the office thinking about the struggles that doctors face. Earlier in the day I had been on phone calls with several docs, each facing different challenges. I was clicking back the conversations in my mind and thinking about how happy each doctor was with the solutions that we developed for each of them. It was a great feeling and as I was basking in that moment, the song "Goin' Nowhere" came on satellite radio.

I sat, somewhat mesmerized, listening to Ashley McBryde sing the lyrics. Very quickly I thought wow, this could be a chiropractic anthem. "Goin Nowhere" is the story of a successful singer that was told that they'd never make it, never be a success, and that singer is now looking back and thanking all the naysayers.

How many times have we as chiropractors been told that we don't belong? That we are not real doctors? That our care is dangerous? That our patient must discontinue care immediately?

Heck, we've been told that women can't be on chiropractic stages because we can't sell seats. That there's not enough value. Well guess what, three powerful women wrote this book that you just bought and are now reading. Now what?

How many times have you been told that you'd never amount to anything? That the world's problems were your fault? That somebody else was responsible for your success?

Well guess what?

Choose to **STOP LISTENING.**

It's your story, your canvas and you get to paint the details. Go ahead, paint a masterpiece. Exceed expectations. In fact, expect to have Peace, Health and Freedom; it's your birthright.

Remember when chiropractors were so principled and so full of belief in the chiropractic principles that they went to jail for them? Where are we now?

If you look carefully, chiropractic is at a precipice: it's either going to explode with success or become extinct. Our choice.

To the destructive voices in chiropractic and against chiropractic...

Choose to **STOP LISTENING.**

Opposition is just that, opposites...not oppression. It's only oppression when we let it be.

Chiropractic has always survived from grassroots support. The principles of chiropractic are so pure that our opposition has never been able to truly suppress us because **CHIROPRACTIC WORKS.**

To all the false science out there...

Choose to **STOP LISTENING.**

Look at the research coming out today validating everything we've empirically known to be true with chiropractic care over the past 100+ years.

Docs, put the blinders on to block out the view of your critics and the headphones on over the nasty voices.

In the words of Richard Branson: "Screw it, let's do it." It's OK to build the practice of your dreams. Change and enhance the life of every lucky patient that walks through the doors of your practice.

Be a part of our profession's exploding success.

Live a life that exceeds your dreams.

In fact, write _your_ own song that celebrates _your_ success!

To receive complementary resources to this book including videos, downloads, audios that will support your practice, we invite you to visit:

www.prosperityprinciplesbook.com/resources

This dynamic page will continue to provide updates that are relevant and actionable for you.

Chapter 51

NUTS AND BOLTS CHECK LIST

"No wise pilot, no matter how great his talent and experience, fails to use a checklist."
– Charlie Munger

Here's a gift to from the Indie Docs to you to help get your practice gliding on the tracks efficiently!

Keep this checklist handy and use it to train staff daily. Staff will do exactly what they want to unless the doctor trains them every single day! They will do things that they think will be helpful when in fact they are not the experts. You are the expert and treat the staff training the same way you'd treat a new patient. TRAIN staff daily.

- ☐ The flow of patients through the office should be simple and consistent. The flow should be so consistent that if the patient is all on their own, they could get from A to B without instruction. There should be multiple sign in capabilities. It doesn't matter if there are kiosks or iPads or some other option; the front desk needs to be able to handle more than one patient signing in.

- ☐ The front desk expert is your quarterback. LEAVE them alone and let them do their job. That doesn't mean they don't need to be trained but it does mean that you need to stay out of the front desk area. Obviously, that excludes problematic situations. Listen to what is happening at the front desk and when there are issues that need the doctor's direction, guidance or a strong hand, you are there in no time.

- ☐ Set up your systems where the patient is pre-paid and pre-booked for the next string of appointments. The patient should know their schedule and have a calendar. If they change their appointments, they receive a new calendar. They should also always get a receipt for the day. This avoids a million problems later!

- ☐ Monthly event calendars for the office should be preprinted and on the front desk for patients with the office phone number on the top. The calendar should have the hours for each day and any planned patient classes, workshops, and/or events. If there is a day of the week that no patients are seen, that is labeled as a training day. The patients need to know that training happens all the time and it isn't a day off at the golf course.

- ☐ There shouldn't be any food, drinks, cell phones or any other distractions visible at the front desk or anywhere else in the office.

- ☐ Every time a patient walks in they should be greeted by name and with a huge smile even if the front desk person is on the phone and this includes the new patient.

- ☐ A separate huge spiral style appointment book should be for new patients and used every single time a new patient schedules an appointment. Their name, phone number, referral source, reason for their appointment should be put in specific new patient time.

- ☐ Send NP forms to the new patient if at all possible so that the new patient appointment is a smooth event.

- ☐ The new patient should never wait longer than 7-10 minutes. If there is an issue, send a staff member directly to the new patient to let them know that the doctor has an emergency patient and will be with them as soon as possible.

- ☐ The time should be put on the new patient chart so the doctor can see when the patient arrived.

- ☐ New patients and reports should be booked on the 30- and 45-minute times out of an hour, i.e. 10:30 and 10:45.

- ☐ The adjustments/re-exams should be pre-booked on the hour and quarter hour, i.e. 10:00, 10;15.

- ☐ When a patient leaves the staff should always tell them that they will see them on their next scheduled appointment and be specific. An example would be: "See you at two on Thursday Mary". This needs to happen from more than one staff member and it's a huge bonus if the doctor says it as well.

- ☐ If a patient wants to stop care, get a refund, can't make a scheduled payment the doctor needs a consult with them immediately. It is best to handle each one of those as fast as possible. Those are Board complaints in the making and it's best to put out that fire as soon as possible.

- ☐ Music is healing and relaxing and should be played at an appropriate level in the office and it shouldn't be distracting.

- ☐ The office should be spotless at all times. Staff is responsible for this every morning and every evening. Checking the bathrooms hourly is an awesome rule.

- ☐ Bathrooms should have plenty of supplies, including hand soap, paper towels, air freshener (essential oils, nothing toxic) and we have a night light as an extra touch for kiddos and seniors so they can find the light switch without any trouble. Rule of thumb for us is that if you wouldn't go in the restroom why would a patient go in there and it needs attention immediately.

- ☐ As the patient makes it to the adjusting area, they should be greeted by name and told where to go. There should be a specific area near the adjusting tables for valuables to be placed securely and definitely not on the floor or under the doctor's feet. As the patient gets up from the adjusting table it is a nice touch for the staff or even the doctor to hand the patient their valuables back. We have plastic bins by each adjusting table just for this.

- ☐ When the patient comes to an adjusting table, the staff should tell them which table to lay down on and the patient should be on the table in the appropriate position when the doctor arrives.

The time frame for the doctor to arrive shouldn't be any longer than 2 minutes. Our staff tells the patient to "lie down, take 4 deep breaths and get ready for an awesome adjustment".

- ☐ The doctor should ALWAYS announce themselves before they touch a patient to adjust them. NO exceptions!

- ☐ If the doctor moves around the table a hand should always be on the patient in an appropriate area so that the patient doesn't have to guess where the doctor is.

- ☐ A staff member should always be with the doctor when patients are getting adjusted.

- ☐ The patient is taught to roll on their side to get up and shouldn't be pulled up by the staff or doctor.

- ☐ When the doctor is checking the patient to adjust them, the doctor should have appropriate table talk and it should include a statement that the patient knows the doctor found the problem for the day. I.e. Doctor is palpating patient and says, "Here it is…I found it", etc.

- ☐ The doctor always lets the patient know that the adjustment is just what they needed and there will be more to come to correct their problems.

- ☐ Move hair, hoodies, and jewelry out of the way during the adjustment.

- ☐ Tables should be cleaned after every patient with a non-toxic sanitizer.

- ☐ It is great to ask the patient what their number 1 problem spot is for the day. There are many reasons for this…one is that you need to document in the notes that the patient "verbally reported…" so that nothing is left off the note for that day. They also may have a new issue that they didn't let the front desk know about and the new issue may need a new diagnosis code, exam or x-ray. What this question does is to connect the doctor to the patient, and it lets the patient know that the doctor isn't robotically going through the adjustment and is well-aware of the patient's problem. This in no way creates a symptom-oriented patient because the doctor is always at the ready to explain the difference between the symptom and the root cause of the symptom. That will keep the patient from being a poor reporter and the doctor up to date on the patient's progress.

- [ ] The doctor can't ignore the patient's main complaint. It must be addressed (symptom/root cause) and touched. NEVER ignore a patient's complaints. For example, the patient says that their knee is hurting. The doctor can look at the knee, touch the knee and tell the patient that the knee pain is a symptom of the lower back problem that they have and will get better as the lower back stabilizes and improves. The doctor must always connect the complaint to the chiropractic issues and let them know that the adjustment is the solution.

- [ ] The staff should always be able to tell the patient what the modalities are for, what to expect when the patient is on the modality and what the modality will accomplish. We train staff that every modality reduces pain, reduces inflammation and helps the body heal.

- [ ] The doctor's table talk is essential to retention. The patient must know why they are coming in and what the goals are for the care plan. For example, "Mary your neck is not moving, that is why it is hurting, and this procedure, the adjustment, is the number one way for us to correct that problem and it will also reduce your pain and eventually make your pain go away long term. Does that make sense, Mary?" It is a conversation not a lecture, so the patient needs to be involved and the more questions that patient answers the more they'll understand why they paid what they paid and why they need to continue their care.

- ☐ Being the doctor means that the patient doesn't tell you what to do, you make the call on where and how the patient gets care. When the patient is hurting, they have a tendency to tell you "push here", "do that one more time to my neck, you didn't get it all", "You didn't adjust me where I hurt, and my back still hurts so adjust/pop me here". This is a patient management issue and should be handled fast and effectively. The patient may not truly understand chiropractic, and if that is the case the doctor needs to step in and explain the principles of how chiropractic works. We keep this explanation short and sweet. For example, "Mary, your spine isn't moving like it should, the nerves are irritated and are not functioning right and that is causing your symptoms. The nerves from your back go to your knee and that is why you feel knee symptoms. We are correcting your spine so that it feels better, works better and your knee will feel better and work better, too. Inch by inch it's a cinch, yard by yard it's hard." This is usually a conversation that happens at the beginning with a new patient when the doctor didn't explain the diagnosis and solution. If it happens with an established patient, the doctor must control that issue immediately and educate the patient.

- ☐ Showing the patient what didn't work on their body before an adjustment and then adjusting the patient then showing them how the body works better after the adjustment is always smart. You don't have to do it every time but if you have a hard to handle patient that needs to know something is better, you need to do it every time. We do several pre-tests and post-tests during visits to show patients their changes. This is a great idea for those tough to handle patients, and it also creates confidence in the doctor from the patient. That patient knows that they are their way to better health, and it isn't just a "howdy doody" visit where nothing was accomplished.

- ☐ Staff huddles/meetings should happen daily, and stats should be addressed daily.

- ☐ At the end of the day, we always ask the staff "who was the happiest patient today?" This question gets so many things accomplished. Some staff may not have heard about a patient's testimonial for that day, it also focuses the staff on the positive events of the day, and they don't get caught up in the one negative thing that happened.

This is a "short list" and by no means does it cover it all. We could actually write a book on Nuts and Bolts Check Lists all by itself! This is a fantastic start so use this daily and personalize it for your office!

Chapter 52

WHERE DO YOU GO FROM HERE?

"Success is not final, failure is not fatal:
it is the courage to continue that counts."
– Winston Churchill

The world truly is your oyster and your ability to be successful in practice and enjoy life is up to you.

Peace. Health. Freedom.

It can all be yours!

Success is conscious choice and a journey that is user defined. The objective of this book is to begin to educate you, raise your awareness and to ask questions to challenge your insight and perspectives.

You may not have all the answers inwardly or at your fingertips presently. That's ok. Powerful information and answers are available to you 24/7 at:

www.ProsperityPrinciplesBook.com/resources

See you there!

ABOUT THE AUTHORS

Dr. Jeri Anderson, DC

Dr. Jeri has been described as a game changer and a rainmaker. She is an out of the box thinker with a huge love for chiropractic. Dr. Jeri is a 1986 graduate of Life Chiropractic College-West and was the 2007 Alumna of the Year. She has earned chiropractic certifications in Sports Injuries and Spinal Trauma. Additionally, Dr. Jeri is a Certified Strength and Conditioning Specialist. She has built highly successful practices in three states.

Dr. Jeri has acted as a state board expert consultant, taught post-graduate content to chiropractors and attorneys, and has delivered expert testimony in the courts.

When not working in the chiropractic space, Dr. Jeri is a passionate advocate for healthy change. She has developed a community vertical aeroponic garden to create healthy food for her patients and their families, and to educate her community about real food. She also enjoys her racking up rides on her Peloton bike.

Dr. Darci Stotts, DC

Dr. Darci Stotts is a pure innovator. Kind, honest, and with a great sense of humor- she is that quiet voice in the room, that when she speaks everyone leans forward to listen. She offers an unparalleled perspective in doctor-patient communication. She graduated from Texas Chiropractic College in 1989 and began her private chiropractic practice in San Angelo, Texas that same year.

The next year, 1990, proved to be a monumental year for Dr. Stotts in that she met her two mentors that she would study under until the present day. She met Dr. Roy Sweat in Atlanta, Georgia, and Dr. Rolla Pennell in Kansas City, Missouri.

Dr. Sweat developed the Atlas Orthogonal adjusting technique that Dr. Stotts uses in practice, and Dr. Pennell was her mentor in the MDC group. Both doctors have been crucial in leading the chiropractic profession into another millennium of success. Dr. Pennell's teachings led Dr. Stotts to take her business of chiropractic and thought processes to another level.

Dr. Stotts became a Board Certified Atlas Orthogonist in early nineties and received her certification in Chiropractic Spinal Trauma around the same time. Dr. Stotts was published in the Texas Chiropractic Journal for her work with the Atlas Orthogonal Technique.

Dr. Stotts continues to write, further her studies, is still in private practice and now mentors to new graduates as well as experienced chiropractors. Her passion is also to see the chiropractic profession grow healthier and more successful. Knowing that the profession is a better, stronger, more stable profession than it was in 1989 is what drives her to share her experiences from the thirty plus years in a rocking, fun practice that still is helping folks gain spinal health and overall wellness.

Patty Dominguez

In 2012, Patty left her cushy job as a Fortune 50 Corporate Executive, managing a billion dollars in marketing spend over her eighteen year career working with the world's biggest consumer goods brands.

She now brings her brilliant strategic thinking coupled with innovative and cutting-edge digital marketing strategies to her clients.

Patty regularly works and hones her skills hand in hand with the prominent faces and titans of internet marketing.

She coaches small business owners on how to maximize their reach with proven marketing principles. Her greatest passion is in helping her clients own their niche and become "*category of one*" status. It is with her signature Prolific Positioning™ and online marketing strategies that her clients reliably elevate their business and root themselves in impact and legacy.

When not working, you can find Patty working real hard at figuring out the whole "work/life balance" myth with her husband and two teenage boys.

Made in the USA
Columbia, SC
29 August 2019